Dr. C. Andrews   Dr. U. Baensch   ·   Tropical Aquarium Fish

© 1993
Tetra-Press
Tetra-Werke Dr. rer nat. Ulrich Baensch GmbH
P.O. Box 1580. D-49304 Melle, Germany
All rights reserved, incl. film, broadcasting, television as well as the reprinting
3rd edition, 1994
Printed in Spain by Egedsa, Sabadell
D.L.B.: 36.634–94

Distributed in the U.S.A. by
Tetra Sales U.S.A.,
3001 Commerce Street
Blacksburg, VA 24060

Distributed in UK by
Tetra Sales, Lambert Court,
Chestnut Avenue, Eastleigh, Hampshire S05 3ZQ
WL-Code: 16002

ISBN 3-89356-131-5

Dr. Chris Andrews

Dr. Ulrich Baensch

Tropical Aquarium Fish

About the Authors:

<u>Dr. Chris Andrews</u> is well known to fish hobbyists around thew world. He is a regular contributor to TV and radio programmes, as well as hobbyist magazines, and has written several books. A specialist in fish diseases and fish breeding, he was Curator of the Aquarium, Reptile House and Insect House at London Zoo, but he now is working at the National Aquarium in Baltimore/USA.

<u>Dr. Ulrich Baensch</u> who, from an early age dedicated his life to the care of fish and plants in the aquarium, is one of the pioneers of the aquarium hobby. It is probably true to say that he actually invented flaked fish foods and without his innovation the upsurge of interest in aquarium fishkeeping would not have been possible.

As a qualified agriculturist and biologist, Dr. Baensch worked for some years in the scientific research field of genetics, later setting up business as an agricultural botanist. At his interest in aquarium fish developed, a hot house of his was turned over the study and culture of fish and plants.

Aware of the importance of diet to the successful maintenance of aquarium fish Dr. Baensch later founded Tetra in the early 1950's and since then the company has been at the fore-front of aquarium fish nutrition and all respects of tank and fish care.

Dr. Baensch has written several other books of fishkeeping and is the editor of the **TI** magazine.

As a result of his many years devotion to the study of fish, the author is able to introduce both newcomers and experienced aquarists into the realms of successful fishkeeping.

Contents

Section One

Section Two

A Catalogue of Popular Aquarium Fish

CHAPTER 1
Introduction

In the beginning

The hobby of ornamental fishkeeping is now incredibly popular, with many millions of dedicated enthusiasts all around the world. The first people to keep fish for ornamental purposes were probably the Romans, although by 350 AD the Chinese had already begun to produce goldfish from a local carp species. With painstaking patience and selective breeding, a whole range of varieties of fancy goldfish were available in China by 1200 AD, by which time goldfish were quite common pets in Chinese homes. Around 1500 AD the goldfish was taken to Japan, where Japanese fish culturists selectively bred the species further.

By way of comparison, koi carp (very much a separate species from the goldfish) first appeared in in Japan around 800 or 1000 AD – again selectively bred from local, but less distinctly marked, carp. By the 1500's, Koi were very popular in Japan, and soon set out to conquer the world.

The first mention of ornamental fish being kept in indoor aquaria in Europe was during the mid-1600's. The fish in question were probably the paradise fish (*Macropodus*) and not, as is often supposed, the goldfish. The first goldfish did not, in fact, appear in this country until around 1700 and soon became a popular addition to fasionable homes of the time.

During the 1800's the idea of a 'balanced' aquarium, containing fish *and* plants, was developed and by 1853 there was a public aquarium at London Zoo. What followed was something of a surge of interest in fishkeeping, with public aquaria appearing in many European cities. Greater numbers of fish species became available and the now familiar tank-bred strains started to appear.

The continental Europeans (especially the Germans) were very important in the development of the tropical side of the hobby, although tropical aquaria were becoming quite popular in a number of other countries around the world by the 1920's.

◀ **Cardinal tetra**

The recession of the 1930's, and then World War II, seemed to have an effect on slowing the growth of interest in ornamental fishkeeping, but with a subsequent upsurge of interest in the 1950's and 1960's. It was during this time that many of the now often quoted (and perhaps misquoted) 'rules' of fishkeeping were laid down. These rules (more guidelines really) are still of some relevance today, but must never be allowed to stifle the adventurous and inquisitive nature of modern day aquarists.

During the 1950's the *Tetra* range of prepared fish diets appeared, meaning that hobbyists no longer had to rely on poor quality live foods or even home-made foods for their fish.

The availability of cheap air travel, wide-bodied jet aircraft and the mass production of ornamental fish on fish farms, along with the development of high quality, reliable aquarium equipment and hardware, have all contributed to the startling popularity of fishkeeping in recent years.

The shape of ornamental fishkeeping

One reason why fishkeeping is so popular must be that the hobby can take many forms, and provide pleasure in many ways. Although within this book we consider the keeping of *tropical* freshwater aquarium fish, the above mentioned goldfish and koi carp (along with a range of other so called 'coldwater' fish) can be kept in unheated aquaria and garden ponds. Furthermore, the dazzling fish and diverse invertebrates from tropical oceans are now providing a whole new dimension to the hobby.

Fishkeeping is certainly relaxing, as the fish are admired as they glide gracefully amongst the tank decor. However, the hobby is also educational, teaching adults and children alike about animals and plants from far-off countries, along with more general biological principles too. Aquarium clubs, with their local, national and even international meetings, also make fishkeeping a

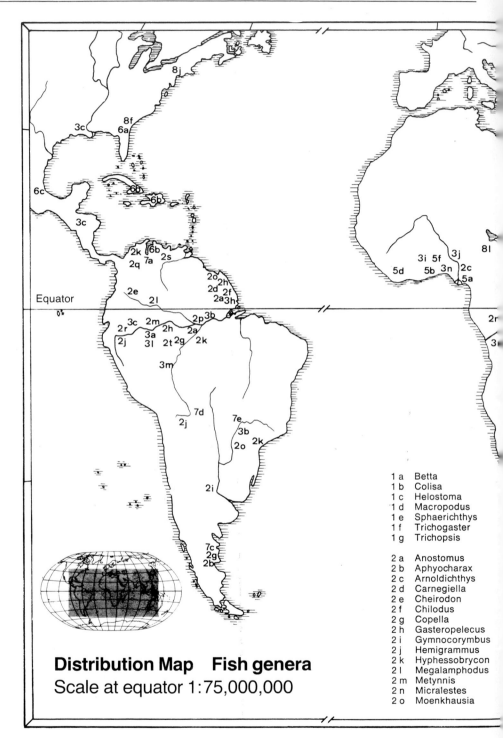

8j

8f
6a
3c

6c

3c

6b

6b

2k 6b 2s
2q 7a

2e   2l

2o 2h
2d 2f
2a 3h

3c 2m 2h
2r   3a   2a
2j   3l 2t 2g   2k

3m

7d
2j

7e
3b
2o 2k

2i

7c
2g
2b

Equator
0°

3i 5f 3j
5d   5b 3n 2c
5a

8l

2r

3

Distribution Map   Fish genera
Scale at equator 1:75,000,000

1 a	Betta
1 b	Colisa
1 c	Helostoma
1 d	Macropodus
1 e	Sphaerichthys
1 f	Trichogaster
1 g	Trichopsis
2 a	Anostomus
2 b	Aphyocharax
2 c	Arnoldichthys
2 d	Carnegiella
2 e	Cheirodon
2 f	Chilodus
2 g	Copella
2 h	Gasteropelecus
2 i	Gymnocorymbus
2 j	Hemigrammus
2 k	Hyphessobrycon
2 l	Megalamphodus
2 m	Metynnis
2 n	Micralestes
2 o	Moenkhausia

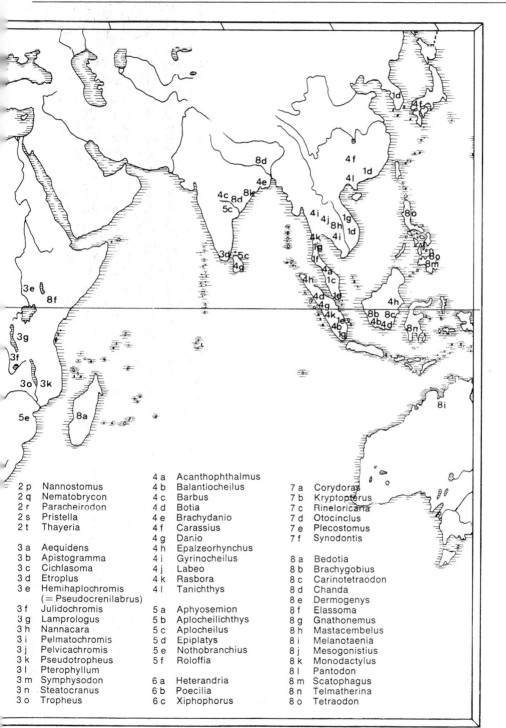

		4 a	Acanthophthalmus			
2 p	Nannostomus	4 b	Balantiocheilus	7 a	Corydoras
2 q	Nematobrycon	4 c	Barbus	7 b	Kryptopterus
2 r	Paracheirodon	4 d	Botia	7 c	Rineloricaria
2 s	Pristella	4 e	Brachydanio	7 d	Otocinclus
2 t	Thayeria	4 f	Carassius	7 e	Plecostomus
		4 g	Danio	7 f	Synodontis
3 a	Aequidens	4 h	Epalzeorhynchus		
3 b	Apistogramma	4 i	Gyrinocheilus	8 a	Bedotia
3 c	Cichlasoma	4 j	Labeo	8 b	Brachygobius
3 d	Etroplus	4 k	Rasbora	8 c	Carinotetraodon
3 e	Hemihaplochromis	4 l	Tanichthys	8 d	Chanda
	(= Pseudocrenilabrus)			8 e	Dermogenys
3 f	Julidochromis	5 a	Aphyosemion	8 f	Elassoma
3 g	Lamprologus	5 b	Aplocheilichthys	8 g	Gnathonemus
3 h	Nannacara	5 c	Aplocheilus	8 h	Mastacembelus
3 i	Pelmatochromis	5 d	Epiplatys	8 i	Melanotaenia
3 j	Pelvicachromis	5 e	Nothobranchius	8 j	Mesogonistius
3 k	Pseudotropheus	5 f	Roloffia	8 k	Monodactylus
3 l	Pterophyllum			8 l	Pantodon
3 m	Symphysodon	6 a	Heterandria	8 m	Scatophagus
3 n	Steatocranus	6 b	Poecilia	8 n	Telmatherina
3 o	Tropheus	6 c	Xiphophorus	8 o	Tetraodon

social activity. The one thing that keeping fish can never be called is boring. There is always another challenge, another species to keep or breed, another observation that perhaps you (and you alone) have made and can pass on to fellow enthusiasts.

Sources of fish

Up until relatively recent years most of the tropical aquarium fish available to hobbyists originated from the wild or (perhaps) had been bred in small numbers by local fish-keepers. Nowadays many of the more popular varieties are bred in enormous numbers on ornamental fish farms or rearing stations, especially in places like Florida (USA) and the Far East. These fish farms do not only breed their own local species, since (for example) Asian *and* South American species are being mass produced on the farms in Hong Kong, Singapore, Thailand, Malaysia and Florida.

Farm produced fish can be more hardy and harbour fewer parasites than wild caught fish, and producing the really popular aquarium species on fish farms also means that wild stocks do not have to be depleted to supply the hobby. Not that all of the fish that aquarists are interested in are (or perhaps can be) bred in this fashion. Thus, the dedicated home aquarist has a real role to play in studying and breeding some of the more delicate or 'difficult' species, thereby adding to our knowledge of these lesser known fish.

Planted community tank in the home

CHAPTER **2**
First Considerations

This book deals specifically with the setting up and maintenance of a tropical freshwater aquarium. When first starting in this branch of the hobby there are a number of basic considerations to take account of, and one or two choices to be made.

The tank

Ready made, good quality aquaria are now available from aquarium shops. Glass tanks are preferred over plastic ones, since the latter are rather easily scratched, which eventually spoils their appearance.

Generally speaking it is a good idea to choose as large a tank as possible, obviously bearing in mind its cost and likely location in the home. A twelve gallon aquarium (say 24 × 12 × 12 ins) should be looked upon as a minimum, although an eighteen gallon tank (say 36 × 12 × 12 ins) is even better. Choosing a larger tank will mean that you can keep a bigger variety of fish and achieve a more pleasing underwater landscape (or 'aquascape'). Furthermore, larger tanks help provide more stable conditions than very small tanks, and are no more difficult to maintain.

Another point to bear in mind is that a tank with a water depth of (say) 15 or even 18 ins will permit more imaginative planting and tank decoration than a tank of 12 ins. This can be quite important if the tank is intended to be a focal point in the home.

CALCULATING TANK VOLUME AND WEIGHT

1. Tank length × width × water depth (all in feet)
   = capacity in cubic feet

   Capacity in cubic feet × 7.5
   = volume in US gallons

   (Capacity in cubic feet × 6.25
   = volume in Imperial gallons)

   In a decorated aquarium, 10% should be deducted from this figure to allow for gravel, rocks, etc.

2. Volume in US gallons × 8.5
   = weight of water in pounds

   (Volume in UK gallons × 10
   = weight of water in pounds)

   The weight of the tank, rocks, gravel, etc, will have to be added to the weight of water to estimate total weight of the fitted, set-up aquarium.

As will be seen from the calculations in the Table, a fitted and decorated aquarium can weigh several hundred pounds, and so will require firm, even support. If a very large aquarium is intended, the structural integrity of the load bearing floor may require investigation, especially if the tank is to be installed in an upstairs room.

Set up tanks – community fish and plants

Siting the tank

The aquarium should be sited where it is to be best appreciated, by both the hobbyist, his/her family, and visitors to their home. The normal viewing height of a television is a good height for an aquarium too.

Direct sunlight, room heaters, and draughts from doors and windows can cause algal problems and/or temperature fluctuations in the aquarium. Similarly fish are easily upset by too much vibration.

Some thought must also be given to the proximity of a suitable power socket (even if the power requirements of an average aquarium are much less than 1000 watts), and that access into the tank (to add and remove water and carry out other items of maintenance) will also be required.

Types of aquarium set-ups

How the rocks, plants and other items of tank decor are arranged is, of course, down to the individual tastes of the hobbyist, although (and as noted later) the fish also have certain requirements in this regard.

It is possible to divide tropical aquaria into two broad types:

* *The community tank* This set-up houses a range of different fish species, chosen because not only do they get on well together, but also because their colour, behaviour and general appearance compliments each other. Real or artificial plants, rock work, bogwood, etc, are all integral parts of most community tanks.

A particular kind of community tank may house fish and perhaps plants from a single

---

FISHKEEPING AT A GLANCE

Correct diet
– Balanced, varied diet based on quality dried foods. Avoid overfeeding. Use only 'safe' live foods.

Temperature
– Avoid sudden changes. 23–26° C (73–79° F) for tropical species.

Compatibility
– Ensure that all fish in the same tank will mix.
– Ensure there are refuges for timid species.
– Keep most fish in pairs or small shoals.

Stocking level
– Allow 10 sq ins of water surface for each inch of fish.

pH
– Avoid sudden changes.
– 6.5–7.5 is satisfactory for most freshwater fish.

Water hardness
– Avoid extreme values for most freshwater fish.

Specific gravity
– 1.002–1.010 for brackish water fish.

Ammonia/nitrite/nitrate
– Negligible ammonia and nitrite in established tanks.
– Nitrate is less important for most freshwater fish.

Plants/lighting
– In freshwater aquaria provide 15–20 watts of a cool white fluorescent lighting or 30–40 watts of tungsten bulb or *Grolux* lighting per square foot of water surface.
– Tanks deeper than 15 ins will require more light than this.
– Leave lights on for 10–14 hours per day.
– Unplanted tanks require less light.

Filtration/Aeration
– Ensure adequate filtration and/or aeration at all times.
– Carry out regular filter maintenance.

Partial water changes
– Remove about 25% of the tank volume every 2–4 weeks, and top up with conditioned water of similar temperature.

Remember
– Regular maintenance ensures healthy fish and plants.

geographical locations, thus recreating a real piece of nature in the home.

* *The species tank* Some hobbyists prefer to establish a tank that only houses a single species of fish, perhaps because it is aggressive or very timid towards other species, or perhaps because it has exacting environmental requirements. Some fish just look best on their own too. Species tanks are also set-up for breeding purposes, even if the fish can be kept in a community tank.

The tank decor (and water quality) in a species aquarium often reflects very closely the behaviour and needs of the resident fish. Scavenger fish (eg catfish) may be included to improve tank maintenance.

Further information

A general outline of the requirements of tropical aquarium fish is provided in the Table. These will all be discussed in more detail in the following chapters, providing all the information necessary to set-up a successful aquarium.

Biotope Tank – Asia

CHAPTER 3

Basic Water Conditions

Fish live in an intimate association with the water around them, and as a result an understanding of basic water chemistry is vital for successful fishkeeping. The creation of special kinds of water conditions (to suit the needs of particular fish species and/or to encourage breeding) is described in Chapter 7. Here is provided an introduction to water chemistry, along with an outline of some of the parameters that are of most relevance to the tropical freshwater enthusiast.

Temperature

The temperature of aquarium water is easily measured and kept within desired limits. Most aquarists should be familiar with the temperature requirements of their fish; 23–26° C (73–79° F) for most tropical species. As noted earlier, an aquarium should never be sited near to a window or close to room heaters since this may, amongst other things, cause dangerous fluctuations in temperature. Many fish can actually survive over a range of temperatures, providing the temperature changes slowly. Every care must be taken to prevent sudden, marked changes in temperature – which can kill fish. Newly acquired fish should be floated inside their plastic bag for about 20 minutes before they are released. This will allow the temperatures to equalise gradually. Aquarium heating is discussed in more detail in Chapter 5.

Dissolved oxygen

Oxygen is vital for the survival of fish, and the dissolved oxygen content of water is affected by both temperature and salinity. At higher temperatures water can effectively hold less oxygen than at lower temperatures, and brackish water and seawater holds less oxygen than freshwater. Symptoms of oxygen shortage are fish gasping at the water surface in a listless fashion. In this situation, about 50 per cent of the water should be removed and replaced with fresh water at the correct temperature. Stocking levels in the aquarium should be examined in case they are too high, and an effective means of aeration installed.

A number of other aspects of poor water quality can also induce symptoms similar to oxygen shortage, highlighting the need for the hobbyist to be familiar with the spectrum of aquarium water quality parameters.

Carbon dioxide

Aquarists are becoming increasingly aware of the importance of carbon dioxide in successful aquarium keeping, especially as a plant fertiliser (see Chapter 5). Excessive levels of carbon dioxide (CO_2) can be toxic to fish, and although CO_2 is produced as part of respiration by all of the tank inmates, high levels are unlikely to build up under normal conditions. This is because CO_2 is taken up by the plants during the daytime and because aeration and the turbulence from the filter easily drive the gas off into the atmosphere.

The effects of aeration on oxygen and carbon dioxide levels in the aquarium are explored more fully in Chapter 4.

OXYGEN LEVELS IN FRESHWATER AND SALTWATER			
Temperature of Water		Saturation Oxygen Level in Milligramsper Litre	
° C	° F	Freshwater	Seawater
10	50	11.3	9.2
20	68	9.2	7.4
30	86	7.6	6.3

As can be seen from the above figures, even when saturated with oxygen (by vigorous aeration) freshwater can effectively 'hold' significantly more oxygen than seawater. However, in both freshwater and seawater, there is a marked decrease of oxygen content with an increase in temperature. Fortunately many tropical freshwater fish can survive in water with quite low levels of oxygen and

A popular aquarium fish – the guppy

some (eg anabantoids) can actually 'breathe' atmospheric air. Most fish, however, must rely on their gills obtaining oxygen from the water.

Acidity or pH

pH is quite simply a measure of the degree of acidity or alkalinity of a solution, or the concentration of hydrogen ions that are present. pH is measured on a scale of 0–14 with pure acid (pH 0) at one end and pure alkali (pH 14) at the other end. A pH of 7 is termed neutral where the acid and alkali are present in equal amounts.

Generally speaking, fish live over the pH range of 5.5 to about 8.5 although within this range different species can have quite different preferences. For example, many of the commonly kept tetras, some dwarf cichlids, discus, etc, prefer a pH on the slightly acid side (pH below 7) whilst others (eg riftlake cichlids and some livebearers) prefer a higher,

more alkaline pH. That is not to say that these fish will only live at these pH values but species such as those mentioned will often only appear at their best and breed if their preferences are noted and provided for.

A very important point about pH is that the scale is not a linear. Therefore, for each single unit change in pH there is a *tenfold* change in the acidity. Thus, if the pH changes from 5 to 6 the acidity changes by a factor of 10. Similarly, if the pH changes from 5 to 7 or 5 to 8 the acidity changes by a factor of 100 (10×10) and a 1000 ($10 \times 10 \times 10$) respectively. Consequently, even quite a seemingly small change in pH (0.5 or 1.0 of a unit) can have quite a dramatic effect on fish, since most species are very sensitive to sudden pH changes. Therefore, every effort must be made to ensure that the fish are not exposed to sudden drastic changes in pH and this will be referred to below.

pH and, as mentioned below, water hardness are easily and accurately measured using test kits from an aquarium shop.

Water hardness

Few subjects within the realms of fishkeeping have caused so much confusion as water hardness, yet it is really quite simple to understand. Water hardness is related to the amount of dissolved salts that are present. Consequently if you live in an area which has predominently limestone or chalk hills, your tapwater is likely to be hard (high in dissolved salts). This is because as the rain percolates through the rocks, it dissolves the soluble magnesium and calcium carbonates and such like which are present.

However, if you live in an area where the surrounding hills are granite or sandstone, the rainwater will not be able to dissolve them so easily, and your tapwater is likely to be soft (eg low in dissolved salts). Rainwater, of course, is itself already soft since it contains few dissolved salts. In some areas your local water company may alter the hardness of your tapwater, or may pipe in water from another locality, and hence the values might not be what you would expect. Hence the need to establish the local water conditions using a reliable test kit.

Water hardness in fishkeeping terms is made up of two components and these are best considered separately.

General hardness (GH) is related to the amounts of calcium and magnesium present, whereas the *carbonate hardness* (KH) is related to the amounts of carbonates/bicarbonates present. Therefore, straightaway we can see that if we add some limestone (which is essentially calcium carbonate) to a sample of water, the GH *and* KH will rise. However, if we add some sodium bicarbonate to the water *only* the KH will rise (since no calcium or magnesium is present).

As with pH, certain fish have certain preferences with regard to water hardness (especially GH) and this can be especially important to their eggs and young fry. Furthermore, KH has an added effect in that it helps to buffer the water thus preventing marked shifts in pH. In freshwater, a KH value of $1-2°$ dH is required to act as a buffer in this fashion.

Water hardness is frequently measured in 'degrees of German hardness' (or $°$ dH). Values below $4°$ dH denote 'soft water', whereas values above (say) $15°$ dH indicate 'hard water'. Some test kits still measure hardness in 'parts per million of calcium carbonate' (or ppm $CaCO_3$), Note that ppm $CaCO_3$ can be converted to $°$ dH by dividing by 17.9.

An indication of the water quality preferences of a wide range of commonly kept aquarium fish is provided later in this book. It must be emphasised that although such conditions may not be essential for the survival of the fish, they may help to improve fish colouration and resistance to diseases, and encourage breeding and good egg and fry survival.

Understanding water analyses

To understand pH and water hardness, some specimen analyses should be carried out as indicated in the Table, using reliable test kits from an aquarium shop.

Rainwater, as collected from a garden butt, is often a little acid (pH 6.3), and relatively low in dissolved salts (low GH, low KH). The use of rainwater for fishkeeping is referred to in detail in Chapter 7.

The tapwater samples measured in the Table were collected from two aquarium shops just twenty miles apart in northern England. The tapwater in area II, being soft and more or less of neutral pH, would be ideal for many of the commonly kept aquarium fish. However, the water in area I is better suited to particularly alkaline preferring, hard water species.

By way of comparison, full strength seawater has a markedly alkaline pH. The high KH and very high GH values are indicative of the large amounts of dissolved salts which are present. The main ingredient of seawater is, of course, sodium chloride (NaCl), although this does not register in any hardness tests. It is the magnesium and calcium salts, and other bicarbonates, which give it its high GH and KH values in seawater.

Cichlids ▶

16

SOME WATER TEST RESULTS

Water \ Parameter	pH	General hardness (GH) °dH	Carbonate hardness (KH) °dH
Rainwater (from butt in garden)	6.3	less than 1	less than 1
Tapwater – area I	7.5	15	11
Tapwater – area II	7.0–7.2	4	3
Marine tank water	8.1–8.2	over 30	8

Pollution in the aquarium

Pollution in the aquarium can be divided into two brand types: 'natural' and 'unnatural'.

Natural pollution arises from fish wastes, uneaten food, plant remains and even dead fish, and can cause elevated levels of potentially toxic ammonia and nitrite, and less toxic nitrate. Such pollutants are, however, normally kept under control by good aquarium management, particularly regular partial water changes and efficient filtration. An established, well maintained aquarium should contain negligible amounts of ammonia and nitrite, although the importance of these pollutants, and the role of filtration in the home aquarium, will be discussed in Chapter 4.

Unnatural pollution in the aquarium can arise from a variety of sources, including insecticide aerosols, paint or tobacco fumes and even the rocks or ornaments that are used as decoration. Keeping aerosols and potentially dangerous fumes away from a tank (and its pumps and filters) is fairly straightforward, and rocks and other aquarium ornaments should be selected with great care or obtained from a reliable aquarium shop. The suitability and safety of items of decor for use in an aquarium can always be investigated by keeping a small number of inexpensive fish in a spare tank with the suspect item for a week or two. Survival of the test fish and normal readings of the pH and water hardness values in the test aquarium, then indicate that the item can probably be used in a set-up tank.

A very important source of potential pollutants in the aquarium is, of course, tapwater. The overall suitability of tapwater, in terms of its pH and hardness values, has already been discussed. However, tapwater can also contain chlorine, chloramine, toxic metals such as copper and (perhaps) insecticides. None of these are present at levels to harm humans, although they can pose a problem for fish.

Chlorine and chloramine are present as a result of the disinfection of the water to make it safe for drinking purposes, and copper and similar metals may arise from household water pipes. Insecticides are used on occasion by water companies, to control pest infestations in the main supply pipes. Abstraction of water from rivers for use in municipal supplies also brings with it certain risks regrading pollution.

Fortunately, chlorine, chloramine and copper and similar metals are easily eliminated using a complete water conditioner, such as *AquaSafe*. Such conditioners are available from aquarium shops, and bring with them a number of other benefits which effectively 'age' new tapwater and make it safe for fishkeeping. It should be noted that in the elimination of chloramine in this fashion, ammonia will be produced. If high levels of ammonia in 'conditioned' tapwater are suspected (which can easily be established using an aquarium test kit), some further treatment of the water may be necessary. Various absorptive resins are available from aquarium shops and these will remove ammonia from freshwater.

Insecticides pose more of a problem. Water companies should publicise when they are adding pesticides such as these to the water supply, so that fishkeepers can avoid using their tapwater for the duration. Filtration of possibly contaminated water over activated carbon for a few hours may be an advantage in this situation, although it is best not to use pesticide treated water for fishkeeping. Fortunately, insecticides are used in this fashion relatively infrequently.

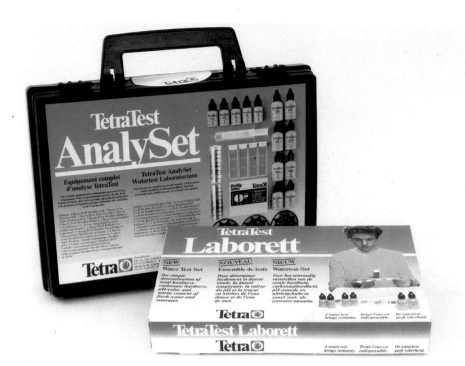

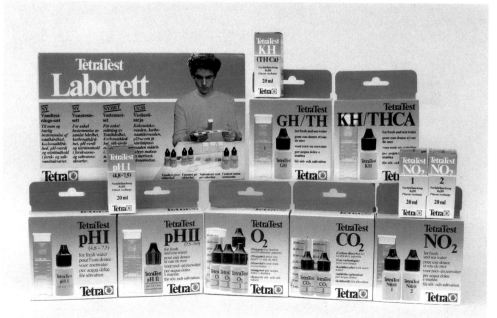

Tetra test kits for water monitoring

CHAPTER 4

Aeration and Filtration

Aeration and filtration are often taken for granted in the modern aquarium, but it is important to realise that different fish and plants have different requirements with regard to aeration and water turbulence, that all filters are not alike, and that all filters do require regular maintenance if they are to perform efficiently.

The processes of aeration and filtration are usually, though not always, carried out by the same piece or pieces of equipment in an aquarium, but for ease of understanding, each process will be considered separately here.

Aeration

Aeration can achieve a number of beneficial effects in the aquarium, and these include:

* improving gaseous exchange with the atmosphere, thereby increasing oxygen levels in the aquarium water. As a result, aeration usually brings about a fall in the carbon dioxide levels in the aquarium too.

* producing the current and/or tubulence favoured by some fish and plants.

* aiding the mixing of the water in the aquarium, preventing the occurrence of 'dead spots' and ensuring an even distribution of heat from the heater-thermostat.

As was noted in Chapter 3, fish (just like other living organisms) need oxygen to survive, but oxygen is far less abundant in water compared to air. In an aquarium, fish, plants and the bacteria and other micro-organisms in the filter and gravel, all use up oxygen and this can be consumed faster than it enters the water from the air above the water surface. High levels of organic matter (uneaten food, plant remains, dietritus, etc) all encourage the growth of micro-organisms, which can unnecessarily deplete oxygen resources in the aquarium too. As will be described in Chap-

ter 5, plants do produce oxygen during the daylight hours (by the process known as 'photosynthesis') which is, of obvious, of benefit to the aquarium as a whole. However, photosynthesis ceases at night when plants become consumers, rather than producers, of oxygen. As a result, simple diffusion of oxygen into the water from the atmosphere, and oxygen production by the aquarium plants, cannot always be relied upon to supply enough oxygen for a healthy aquarium, especially if it is heavily stocked with fish.

Various aeration devices are available (eg airpump with airline and airstone, spray bar from a power filter, the outlet tube from an undergravel or polyfoam filter) and these will aid oxygen uptake by the aquarium water. This is achieved by the bubbles from an airstone releasing oxygen into the water as they rise in the water, but more importantly by increasing water turbulence at the water surface, thereby encouraging gaseous exchange with the atmosphere.

However, too much turbulence can be detrimental. Over vigorous aeration can deplete the carbon dioxide from the water which may be needed by plants as a food source. Furthermore, not all fish and plants require very turbulent water conditions, as many of the commonly kept aquarium varieties actually originate from still or quite slow flowing waters. Therefore, as a guide most tropical freshwater aquaria probably receive sufficient aeration via their filter(s), although an additional airstone (adjusted to produce a gentle stream of bubbles) can aid general water circulation.

If an oxygen deficiency is going to occur, it will often be in very heavily stocked tanks, in tanks that are poorly maintained and which contain large amounts of organic debris, or in heavily planted tanks during the night when photosynthesis ceases. As a result, aeration deviced (and filters) must never be turned off for long periods, and certainly left running overnight.

The Nitrogen Cycle

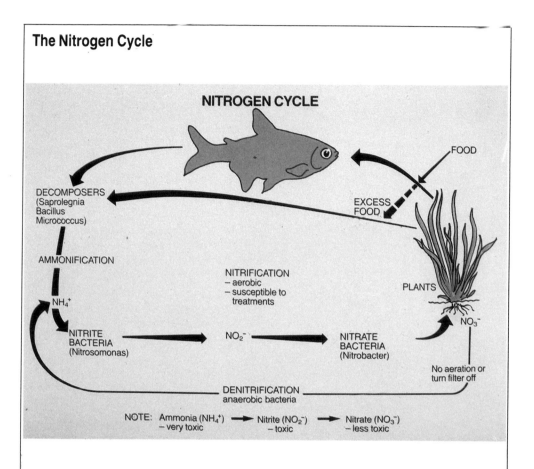

NITROGEN CYCLE

FOOD

DECOMPOSERS
(Saprolegnia
Bacillus
Micrococcus)

EXCESS
FOOD

PLANTS

AMMONIFICATION

NITRIFICATION
– aerobic
– susceptible to
treatments

NH_4^+

NO_3^-

NITRITE
BACTERIA
(Nitrosomonas)

NO_2^-

NITRATE
BACTERIA
(Nitrobacter)

No aeration or
turn filter off

DENITRIFICATION
anaerobic bacteria

NOTE: Ammonia (NH_4^+) → Nitrite (NO_2^-) → Nitrate (NO_3^-)
– very toxic   – toxic   – less toxic

Uneaten food, plant remains and fish waste give rise to ammonia. *Nitrosomonas* bacteria attack the ammonia and convert it to nitrite (NO_2^-), which is attacked by *Nitrobacter* bacteria and results in nitrate (NO_3^-). Nitrate can be used as a fertiliser by plants. The above process of converting ammonia to nitrate is termed 'nitrification' and is aerobic, requiring oxygen. As a result, turning aquarium filters off for long periods can starve these helpful bacteria of oxygen and slow the whole process down. If the filter is left off for a prolonged period, anaerobic conditions may develop, with a complete lack of oxygen. This favours a different group of bacteria, which can actually convert nitrate back to toxic ammonia (by a process called 'denitrification'). For obvious reasons, filters should never be turned off for

longer than an hour or so, and regularly maintained to ensure adequate water flow and oxygen levels within their medium or media.

As a rough guide, aquarium water should contain less than 0.2 milligram/litre of ammonia or nitrite (measured as nitrogen, using a reliable test kit). Nitrate levels are not so critical in freshwater aquaria and quite high levels can be tolerated by most freshwater fish. As will be mentioned in Chapter 6, high levels of ammonia and nitrite frequently occur in newly established tanks. Also, some disease treatments (especially certain antibiotics and methylene blue) can have an adverse effect on the bacteria responsible for converting ammonia to nitrate. Consequently, such treatments need to be used with care in a set-up aquarium.

Filtration

The principle aims of filtration in a tropical freshwater aquarium are:

* removal of suspended matter to encourage clear water conditions.

* control of levels of potentially toxic ammonia and nitrite, which can result from an accumulation of fish wastes, uneaten food, etc.

* treatment of the water to remove other unwanted substances or to achieve certain water conditions.

* water circulation and aeration.

Of the many different types of filter which are used in aquarium fishkeeping, three have gained wide acceptance by hobbyists. These are *undergravel filters, power filters* and *polyfoam filters*.

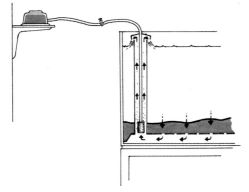

Undergravel filtration draws water through a two to four inch layer of coarse gravel, whereupon the water is both mechanically and biologically cleaned.
Note that the flow of air from the airstone should be adjusted to produce a steady (*not* violent) stream from the uplift tube.

Undergravel filters consist of a perforated filter plate which is placed over most or all of the tank floor, and which is then covered with a two to four inch layer of coarse (say 1/8th ins) gravel. Airlift tubes, powered by airstones from an airpump, draw water down through the gravel (which acts as the filter medium), cleansing the water as it passes through. As the filtered water is drawn up the airlift tube it is aerated before return to the aquarium proper. Neat and unobstrusive, undergravel filters are very popular. The gravel strains or mechanically filters the water, trapping any suspended matter. Within the gravel bed, a rich population of helpful bacteria develops, which breaks down potentially toxic ammonia through nitrite to much less toxic nitrate. Nitrate is, in fact, a food source for plants and algae. This biological conversion of ammonia to nitrate via nitrite is part of the 'nitrogen cycle' which is described in the Figure.

With time the gravel bed of an undergravel filter will become clogged with accumulated debris. This can be prevented by regular use of a combined siphon tube and gravel washer, such as the *HydroClean*. Such gravel washers are available from aquarium shops and enable the gravel to be cleaned without having to completely empty and refurbish the tank. As an alternative to a gravel washer, the top half inch or so of the gravel bed can be gently disturbed and the accumulated debris removed using a standard siphon tube. Maintenance like this must be carried out at least once a month, or there will be a gradual decline in aquarium conditions.

Nowadays, powerheads (electrically driven water pumps) are available that will connect to the top of an undergravel filter uplift tube, and achieve a high turnover through the gravel, with much less noise than from the usual airpump and airstone arrangement. Some powerheads also come with integral aeration devices.

A further refinement to the undergravel filter involves using a modified power filter (see below) to pre-filter the water and then pass it down the uplight tube(s). The water is then forced up through the gravel bed. This 'reverse flow' undergravel filtration has the advantage that debris does not accumulate in the gravel and hence it requires less frequent cleaning.

box. Some power filters are designed to be used inside the aquarium, completely submerged in the water, whilst others are placed at the side of the tank, with pipes bringing water to and from the filter. Power filters are available in a huge range of sizes, but as a rough guide for a tropical community aquarium, the water should be turned over by the power filter several times in a 24 hour period. As has been noted, over vigorous turbulence from some power filters, especially in small aquaria, may have detrimental effects on certain fish and plants.

The most commonly used filter medium for a power filter is a foam insert. This provides an effective way to mechanically clean the water, with large populations of helpful filter bacteria developing within the foam at the same time. Thus the foam insert takes on the role of the gravel in an undergravel filter. Maintenance of this type of medium is very simple: just remove the foam insert and rinse

A simple siphon tube such as this can be used to remove water, as well as accumulated debris, from the aquarium. However, gravel washers like the *HydroClean* are much more efficient at cleaning the gravel.

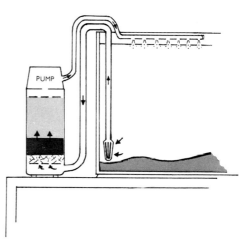

Some hobbyists claim that undergravel filters may have a detrimental effect on plant growth. However, any such negative results can be offset by planting the plants in small pots or trays of compost and then burying these in the gravel. Mixing any kind of compost, fine sand, etc, with the gravel of an undergravel filter will, of course, encourage clogging and must be avoided.

Power filters usually consist of a high turnover water pump which draws water through one or more types of filter media, all of which is enclosed in a neat self contained

Power filters are available which sit inside as well as (like this type) outside the aquarium. Always try and site the inlet and outlet tubes as far apart as possible, to encourage good water conditions. Power filters such as this can be used to turn an 'ordinary' undergravel filter into a reverse flow system, by using the power filter outlet to force water *down* the undergravel uplift. Special attachments are available from aquarium shops.

23

in lukewarm water every 2–4 weeks. This is also a good opportunity to clean all the filter tubes, the filter body, etc, with a soft brush or cloth.

In addition to their potentially high turnover, which can be useful for large tanks or when keeping large, messy fish, various other types of filter media add another dimension to power filters. Nylon wool and porous pot rings are often used as two basic media, although coarse gravel can be substituted for the rings (see Figure). Additional media (like peat, to lower the pH, as will be described in Chapter 7, and aquarium carbon, to remove chemicals like disease treatments from the water) are sometimes used, and various zeolite compounds are now available that will remove ammonia from newly established aquaria, or from aquaria experiencing high ammonia levels for some other reason. Such media, with the resultant filtration possibilities, can turn power filters into miniature 'water treatment plants' for the home aquarium.

Polyfoam filters are available in a number of different types, shapes and sizes. They all

Tetra filters in several sizes

FILTER FACTS

* Small to medium sized tropical community tanks . . .
Polyfoam or power filtration

* Large community tanks . . .
Undergravel or power filtration

* Large messy fish . . .
Power filtration

* Never turn filters off for long periods: they are best left running all the time.

* All filters must be regularly maintained.

* Most fish and plants do not require excessive water turbulence; very noisy filters are likely to be wrongly set-up or need adjusting.

* Filtration (and aeration) does not replace the need for regular partial water changes, 25% every 2–4 weeks.

* Some disease treatments may adversely effect the filter bacteria, and cause a rise in ammonia or nitrite. Use with care and carry out a partial water change, if necessary.

* Filtration over aquarium carbon will remove most disease treatments from the water.

operate, when connected to an airpump, by gently drawing the aquarium water through one or more foam cartridges, where the suspended debris is trapped and where the helpful filter bacteria set about converting ammonia to nitrite and then nitrate. Once again, the foam is acting like the gravel of an undergravel filter.

Good quality filters of this type utilise foam with an enormous internal surface area, that is also extremely durable and, of course, nontoxic to fish. In addition, the filtering capacity of certain models can be increased by the addition of extra cartridges. As with all types of filters, polyfoam filters will require regular attention if they are to perform efficiently. In this instance, the foam cartridge should be rinsed in lukewarm water once every 2–4 weeks, and the filter cartridge renewed every year or so (although the filter cartridges of some cheaper types may require more frequent renewal).

Which filter for your tank?

Undergravel filters are very popular in tropical community tanks, and are likely to remain so. However, efforts must be made to limit any adverse effects of this type of filtration on plant growth, and the above mentioned gravel cleaning process, although essential, can be disruptive in small tanks. As a result, one or more polyfoam filters or a small to medium sized power filter is recommended for most community tanks up to (say) three feet long.

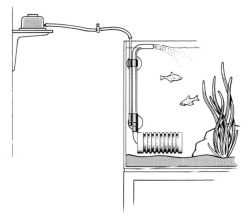

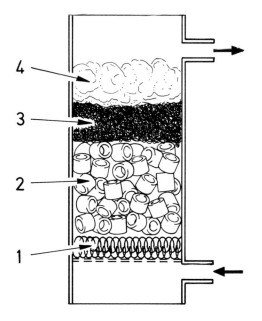

Polyfoam filters are an ideal way to filter small to medium sized tanks. Note that whenever an airpump is used in conjunction with an aquarium, it should be situated above the water level to prevent back siphoning. Inline valves are, however, also available to prevent pump damage as a result of this occurrence.

As the size of the tank increases above this, more powerful power filters or (perhaps) undergravel filtration, should be used. The gravel washing maintenance procedure of undergravel filters is less disruptive in larger tanks, although undergravel filters are unlikely to be adequate for large, messy fish (eg large cichlids, barbs and anabantoids). Good power filtration is almost obligatory when keeping this type of fish in the home aquarium.

At the other end of the scale, in small quarantine and/or breeding tanks, polyfoam filters are ideal. They are easy to set up (and strip down), as well as being efficient without posing any threat to small fry. Combining power filtration with reverse flow undergravel filtration (where a power filter forces water *down* the uplift tube of an undergravel filter, and *up* through the gravel bed) is, however, an excellent, all round though much under used method of filtration that is applicable to many different kinds of aquarium fishkeeping, and should be explored more frequently by hobbyists.

Various filter media can be used in a power filter. Here water is passed through coarse filter wool (1), to remove any crude debris, before flowing over porous pot rings (2) where the large surface area will encourage the bacteria responsible for nitrification. Although not essential, this filter also utilises a layer of carbon (3), but peat or zeolite could also be used at this point. The water finally passes through fine nylon wool (4) to achieve optimum clarity.

CHAPTER 5
Heating, Lighting and Plants

Heating

As already mentioned, tropical freshwater aquarium fish generally require a steady, warm temperature in the range 23–26° C (73–79° F), although some species (eg discus, *Symphysodon*) prefer warmer temperatures around 28–30° C or 82–86° F, whilst others (eg. some killies and barbs) will tolerate cooler temperatives, around 20° C or 68° F. The temperature requirements of individual species of aquarium fish are detailed later in this book. However, since fish are 'ectothermic', and take their body temperature

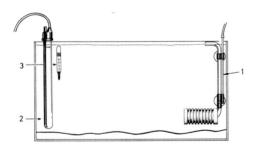

Ideal arrangement of the filter (1), heater-thermostat (2) and thermometer (3) in a small community aquarium.

from their surroundings, it is not only important to provide the correct temperature, but also to prevent fish from being exposed to fluctuating or suddenly changing temperatures. In fact, many of the commonly kept fish will live at a range of water temperatures, so long as the temperature does not fluctuate too frequently or too widely.

Nowadays very stable water temperatures can be provided using a good quality heater-thermostat from an aquarium shop. As a rough guide allow 5–10 watts of heating for

each gallon of water. In a warm or centrally heated room, the lower figure will be enough, whilst in a cooler room (or a room only periodically heated) the higher allowance is recommended. Thus a 20 gallon aquarium will require a 200 watt heater-thermostat, unless the room is centrally heated, when a 100 watt device will probably be sufficient. In larger tanks it is always best to install (say) two or three lower wattage heater-thermostats, rather than a single high powered one. This will not only ensure a better distribution of temperature in the tank, but also mean that it is much less likely for several heater-thermostats to fail at one time and cause a serious drop in temperature. If there is a temporary fault in the heating system (eg as a result of a power cut) the tank can be insulated using polystyrene or even blankets around its front, back and sides. In any event, a heating failure of just a few hours is unlikely to produce a precipitous fall in the water temperature, and a gradual decrease, followed by a gradual increase when the heating comes on again, will not cause too much harm.

The preferred arrangement of the heater-thermostat, thermometer and (polyfoam) filter is shown in the Figure. In large tanks, airstones placed below the heater-thermostat(s) will help ensure good distribution of the heat they produce.

Naturally the correct functioning of the aquarium heating equipment should be checked on a daily basis using a reliable thermometer. Most heater-thermostats can also be adjusted, to some extent, to control the amount of heat they produce.

Lighting

If live plants are not included in the aquarium, the fish will probably thrive at normal room light levels, perhaps turning on an above tank light for viewing for a few hours each day. However, since most hobbyists (especially those with community aquaria)

Metal halide or mercury vapour lamps are excellent for plant growth, but do generate a lot of heat. For this reason they are often suspended well above open topped tanks.

want to grow plants, special attention must be paid to lighting. Natural daylight and sunlight is generally too unpredictable to guarantee good results with aquarium plants and hence some form of above tank artificial lighting system will have to be utilised.

For tanks with a *water depth of less than 18 inches* fluorescent tubes and/or tungsten light bulbs can be used, and are easily installed into the hood or lid of the aquarium. As a rough guide, each foot length of aquarium requires about 40 watts of tungsten bulb lighting or 15–20 watts of cool white fluorescent tube lighting. Some fluorescent tubes are available that have been developed especially to encourage plant growth. However, if *Gro-Lux* (or one of its equivalents) is used, the above flourescent tube allowance should be increased to about 30 watts per foot length of aquarium. Quite pleasing effects can be created using tubes of different spectral (light) qualities in combination with each other, but take care that enough light is provided for the plants.

Of course, tungsten bulbs are cheaper to install than fluorescent tubes, but the former are more expensive to run and do generate quite a lot of heat (which may be undesirable in very small tanks).

Good water circulation (from an airstone or filter) will help to prevent a build up of temperature at the water surface. However, as a general rule, tanks less than 18 inches long will require less than the light allowance which is indicated above, and cooler running fluorescent tubes are then preferred to tungsten bulbs.

For tanks with a *water depth of more than 18 inches* ordinary fluorescent tubes and tungsten bulbs rarely produce enough light to encourage luxuriant plant growth. In this situation, mercury vapour or metal halide lamps are recommended. These are available as attractive pendant fittings which hang about a foot or so above the water surface, although some such lamps are available in specially fan-cooled hoods. Both these types of lamps produce a great deal of heat, but also

27

provide a light that is not only powerful but very good for plants. Although available in a range of wattages, lamps in the range 80–150 watts are normally sufficient for most freshwater aquaria, with each lamp (if positioned according to the manufacturers instructions) capable of illuminating several square feet of water surface to the benefit of the plants beneath.

Fluorescent tubes and mercury vapour and metal halide lamps, will require regular renewal, or the quality and quantity of light that they produce gradually deteriorates with time. Most of these tubes and lamps come with instructions regarding their efficient lifespan. As a rough guide, most will need replacing every 9–12 months.

In addition to the quality and quantity of light for aquarium plants, the daylength is important too. Since most aquarium plants originate from the tropics, the aquarium lights should be left on for between 10–14 hours per day.

Plants

Plants are a decorative as well as a useful addition to a tropical aquarium. They provide shelter, concealment and (on occasion) even food for the fish, although it is the process of 'photosynthesis' that is especially interesting to aquarists.

Just like other living organisms, plants 'respire' twenty four hours a day, that is to say that they are continually taking in oxygen and producing carbon dioxide. However, plants can also 'photosynthesise', which means that under bright light they take in carbon dioxide (and use it as a food source) and liberate oxygen. Thus in terms of the uptake and production of carbon dioxide and oxygen, photosynthesis can be thought of as the reverse of respiration. It is important to note

It is important to position single lights to the front of the aquarium hood, thus illuminating the fish to their best advantage and casting their shadow towards the rear of the tank.

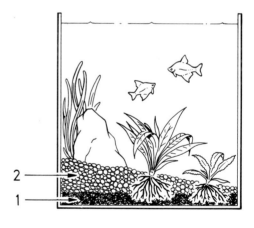

Placing a thin layer of aquarium peat (1) beneath a layer of well washed aquarium gravel (2) is an excellent way to encourage good plant growth. Other gravel fertilisers are also available from aquarium shops.

that, generally speaking, plants release far more oxygen from photosynthesis than they take in as part of respiration, and thus there is (during a 24 hour period) a net production of oxygen. This can be of obvious benefit to the aquarium and its fish. However, to avoid any possibility of a serious depletion of oxygen (or build up of carbon dioxide) overnight, when plants stop photosynthesising, it is important to leave any filter and/or aeration devices running all the time. In fact the filter(s) serving an aquarium must be left running more or less continuously for other reasons too, as was discussed in Chapter 4. Algae, as well as more 'typical' aquarium plants, also photosynthesise, which is one reason why an aquarium may need additional aeration during, and immediately following, the use of an in-tank algicide, or the natural die-back of an algal bloom.

Since carbon dioxide (which is chemically acidic) is used up by the process of photosynthesis it is not surprising that the pH in a planted aquarium may fluctuate to some extent during a 24 hour period, being at its highest (most alkaline) in the afternoon and lowest (most acid) in the early hours of the morning. This type of small, regular fluctuation in pH is quite normal, and does not pose any problems for the fish. However, there is a tendency that, with time, the plants may actually 'use up' the carbonate hardness (KH) in aquarium water to supply CO_2 for their photosynthetic needs. Thus over a period of (say) several weeks there may be a steady overall increase in the average pH value in the aquarium. This is more serious, especially if acid loving fish are kept, but can usually be avoided by regular partial water changes.

Real plants will only thrive if attention is given to general aquarium conditions, especially lighting.

As with fish, certain aquarium plants have preferred conditions with regard to water temperature, pH and hardness and details of these requirements can be found in specialist books on aquarium plants. As a general rule, however, most of the commonly available aquarium plants should thrive so long as extremes of water chemistry are avoided. Nonetheless, plants such as *Echinodorus, Hygrophila* and *Vallisneria* will tolerate the harder, more alkaline conditions which are prevalent in some areas.

To encourage good plant growth, a two or three inch layer of gravel on the aquarium floor can be used to conceal a thin layer of aquarium peat mixed with unfertilised garden soil (see Figure). Naturally a layer of plant compost such as this cannot be used in an aquarium that utilises undergravel filtration, as the compost will clog the filter bed. In any event many hobbyists claim that plants in a tank with undergravel filtration will grow better if planted in s shallow pot or tray containing compost, which is (in turn) buried in the gravel.

Good, routine aquarium care (eg regular filter maintenance, removal of accumulated debris from tank floor, regular partial water changes) will also encourage plant, as well as fish, health. In addition various liquid, tablet and pellet aquarium plant fertilisers are available, whose use can be beneficial in the home aquarium too. Never use fertiliser (or composts) developed for other purposes in the aquarium unless you know it is safe to do so, as disasterous changes to the water chemistry may occur.

With regard to fertilisers, it is not surprising, bearing in mind what was said above concerning photosynthesis, that the addition of carbon dioxide to the water can be used to encourage plant growth. Carbon dioxide diffusers are available from specialist aquatic shops, but must be used according to the manufacturers instructions (especially in soft acid water) to avoid undesirable water quality changes and possible side effects to the fish. Furthermore, it is important to only use a diffuser that has been developed for aquarium use, rather than any other kind of diffuser.

Which plants for your tank?

Most hobbyists will be aware that there are some excellent plastic (imitation) aquarium plants that are now available, and these can be very useful when keeping very destructive fish (eg some cichlids) or fish which enjoy feeding on plants (eg silver dollars, *Metynnis*, etc). However, little can compare with the natural beauty of a community aquarium stocked with real plants. A large range of such plants can be obtained from good aquarium shops, but try to avoid specifically marsh or bog plants, many of which do not thrive if grown totally submerged for too long.

Some general hints on a number of the commonly available aquarium plants are provided in the Table. Note that aquarium plants can be divided into long leaved varieties (such as some *Vallisneria* and *Sagittaria*) which can be used to form a natural backcloth at the rear of the tank, bunch or specimen plants (like *Cabomba* and *Hygrophila*, and large *Echinodorus* and *Cryptocoryne*) for the middle regions of the tank, and small varieties of *Vallisneria*, *Cryptocoryne* and *Echinodorus* to fill the aquarium foreground.

Some further information on planting and tank decor is provided in Chapter 6, although it is important to emphasise the need to take account of the growth potential of aquarium plants when arranging them in the tank.

Plastic plants can be used in the aquarium.

SOME COMMON AQUARIUM PLANTS

Aponogeton crispus South-east Asia	An ideal specimen plant, or a plant for the middle regions of the tank. Prefers a rich compost.
Bacopa carolineana North America	Plant in bunches in the middle regions of the tank.
Cabomba – various species Tropical America	Another 'bunch' plant, useful for the middle or rear tank regions. Needs to be well illuminated.
Crinum thaianum Onion plant South-east Asia	Similar in appearance to giant *Vallisneria*, this tolerant plant is ideal for the rear regions of deep tanks.
Cryptocoryne – various species South-east Asia	Large varieties are useful plants for the middle to rear tank areas. May need bright light
Cryptocoryne nevillii Dwarf cryptocoryne	An excellent foreground plant that required bright light. Other dwarf varieties exist too.
Echinodorus – various species Amazon swords Tropical South America	Large varieties are useful specimen plants, and are usually tolerant of a wide range of conditions.
Echinodorus tenellus Pygmy Amazon sword North and South America	Use as a foreground plant, although some larger varieties of this species occurs. Bright, illumination is required.
Egeria densa South and Central America	A plant to be used in bunches in the rear regions of the tank. Bright, illumination is required.
Hygrophila polysperma Dwarf hygrophila South-east Asia	A hardy plant for the aquarium background. Very tolerant, but provide bright light.
Ludwigia – various species Tropical regions	Very versatile plants, best used in bunches in the middle to rear tank areas.
Microsorium pteropus Java fern South-east Asia	A very hardy and decorative plant that is best grown attached to a piece of rock or bogwood.
Nomaphila stricta South-east Asia	A background plant that is very tolerant of water conditions. Bright light is needed.
Sagittaria platyphylla Giant arrow wort North America	Use as a background, or if planted in groups, a centre-piece plant. Needs a rich substrate and good lighting.
Sagittaria – various species Dwarf arrow wort North America	A number of smaller species are ideal for the middle to foreground regions.
Synema triflorum Water wisteria South-east Asia	Plant in bunches in the rear regions of the tank. Bright illumination is required.
Vallisneria – various species Eel grass, Vallis Europe, now worldwide	Many different species, from giant vallis for the background regions of the tank, to small varieties suitable for the foreground.
Vesicularia dubyana Java moss South-east Asia	A very tolerant plant. Best grown attached to a rock or bogwood.

CHAPTER **6**
Setting up
and Maintenance

Tanks for a tropical community of freshwater fish and plants are available in a range of shapes and sizes. Here we consider in detail the setting up or a 24 × 24 × 15 inch aquarium, although the procedures are similar for tanks larger of smaller than this. Of course, alterations would have to be made to the type and size of the equipment (especially the filter[s], heater[s] and lighting system[s]), as has been discussed in earlier chapters.

Setting up the tank

Having carefully read through the information provided elsewhere in this book, you can now begin settng up your aquarium.

A 'shopping list' of all your initial requirements is provided in the Table. A tank measuring 24 × 12 × 12 (or 15) inches (deep) is probably the smallest which can be set up and easily maintained. Larger tanks are, in fact, even easier to maintain. Very small tanks can be rather troublesome as they are more prone to overstocking, and more susceptible to outside influences (eg temperature fluctuations).

Bring all the equiment in the list home and wash the tank out with clean warm water and a soft (detergent and disinfectant free) cloth. Next two or three polystyrene ceiling tiles should be placed where the tank will be situated; these will form a firm but even base for the aquarium.

The backcloth especially bought for the purpose (although a length of aluminium kitchen foil will also do the job) is now stuck to the outside of the back of the aquarium – held in place with double-sided sticky tape. The backcloth will help create the illusion of a natural underwater aquascape.

Now the tank can be placed on top of the ceiling tiles, and the tiles trimmed back to fit the tank base precisely. Leaving the tank in position, the time has come to wash the gravel. Although a rather laborious and time consuming task, it is worth doing well, since

new gravel is invariably very dusty and dirty. Half a bucket of gravel at a time is rinsed in cold water, until no nore dust or debris can be washed out.

It is also important to ensure that the gravel (as well as any rocks or stones used as decorations) is 'limestone free', unless it is intended for use in a tank for specifically hard water fish. Gravel rich in limestone will cause the pH and hardness in a freshwater aquarium to rise, often outside the preferred range of many of the commonly kept tropical freshwater fish and plants. Local aquarium shops should be able to supply suitable gravel and rocks, although there is a very simple test to determine whether they are likely to produce an increase in the aquarium pH and/or hardness. Just place several drops of vinegar onto the rock or some pieces of gravel. If any small bubbles are produced within a minute or so, then limestone is almost certainly present.

As well as the gravel, any rocks or pieces of bogwood for the aquarium must also be well washed before use. Bogwood will often release substances that colour the water rather brown. In some circumstances (eg when keeping some South American fish which normally inhabit 'brown water' rivers and streams) this can be desirable and even aesthetically pleasing. However, if this effect is considered to be undesirable, it can be reduced (or even prevented) by repeatedly boiling and rinsing the piece of bogwood, or by coating it with several layers of clear polyurethane varnish. Once the varnish is completely dry, the bogwood must be well rinsed before being used in the aquarium. Since bogwood usually has a tendency to float, it can be prevented from doing so by securing it to a piece of flat stone with aquarium sealer or fishing line.

Some hobbyists are inclined to decorate their tanks with a huge assortment of items, some of which may adversely affect the water chemistry – and even the fish and plants. Generally speaking it is best to obtain your items of tank decor from a good aquarium shop. On the other hand, suspect items of

decor can always be 'tested' in a small tank with a few inexpensive fish for a week or two, before being used in the main aquarium.

Returning to the setting-up of the aquarium, before adding the now clean gravel, rocks, etc, to the tank it is vital to check the

SETTING UP AN AQUARIUM*

Aquarium, 24 × 12 × 15 inches (plus stand if required)
Aquarium hood and condensation tray
Gravel (30–40 lbs)
Rocks, bogwood, small flower pots (for decoration)
Two hand nets
Algae scraper
Airline and in-line connector and control valves
Polyfoam filter
Airstone
Aquarium peat (2–3 small bags)
Airpump
Heater-thermostat (100–150 watts) (with holder)

Thermometer
Fluorescent light (2 × 20 watt tubes) and starter units
Electrical plugs
Plants weights
Aquarium junction box (for wiring)
Aquarium backcloth (if required)
Aquarium siphon tube or gravel washer
Bucket(s)
Polystyrene ceiling tiles (2–3)
Tests kits to measure pH, water hardness, ammonia and nitrite levels.

* Note that this list refers specifically to a 24 × 12 × 15 inch tank

positioning of the aquarium. Once it is filled (especially after the water is added), it can be extremely difficult and hazardous to attempt moving the tank. In fact, aquaria that are full of water must never be moved, but at least half emptied first. Therefore, before going any further, check the positioning of the tank on the ceiling tiles, and also check that there is sufficient access behind the aquarium.

Next the aquarium peat should then be mixed with some garden soil, taking care to avoid soil which has been fertilised or chemically treated in any other way in the recent past. The soil-peat mixture should then be spread over the rear two-thirds of the base of the tank, where it will form a rich compost for the plants. On top of this the washed gravel can be carefully laid, to form a layer about one inch deep at the front and three inches deep at the back. Alternatively gravel additives to encourage the growth of plants, are available from aquarium shops.

When first filling the tank, the water should be poured onto a dish or polythene sheet. This will prevent disturbing the tank decor too much.

The aquarium decor can now be added. One or two half buried flowerpots can make interesting looking 'caves'. Rocks from the garden can be used, although it is important to avoid those which contain limestone, since (as mentioned above) these may affect pH and also increase water hardness.

The tank is now ready for filling with water. To prevent undue disturbance of the

gravel whilst filling the tank, a shallow dish should be laid on the tank floor. The tank can then be slowly filled via a hosepipe or jug with water from the cold tap (see Figure). While the tank is slowly filling, it is a good opportunity to connect up the rest of the aquarium equipment: heater-thermostat, airpump, filter and airstone, and lighting. An aquarium junction box is extremely useful at tidying up the electrical wiring. They are available from most aquarium shops. All the electrical equipment should come with full installation instructions which must, of course, be followed closely. The heater-thermostat must never be turned-on unless it is completely immersed in water. Furthermore, the use of a clear glass or perspex condensation tray between the lighting tubes and the water surface will help to reduce water loss through evaporation, splashing onto the tubes and, of course, condensation. Many tank hoods come complete with well fitting condensation trays.

When the tank is about three-quarters full, and the heater-thermostat and filter and airstone positioned in the tank. The filter should be placed in one rear corner, and the airstone in the other, as this will ensure good water circulation throughout the tank. Before topping-up the tank with water, it is a good idea to check that all the equipment is working properly. Removal or rearrangement of any of the equipment can be rather messy once the tank is full of water. The most likely pieces of equipment that will require adjustment are the airstone and filter, where the pump should produce a steady stream of bubbles out of both. Assuming all is well, the thermometer can be stuck to the front glass, and the hosepipe turned back on to top-up the tank with water.

With the tank full, the airpump, junction box and lighting starter units should be placed somewhere safe (where they will not be interfered with, and where there is no danger of contact with water spills or leakages). All the equipment should be left on for at least 24 hours and then the temperature checked, and the air flow through the airstone and filter (again) adjusted if necessary.

Now is a good time to measure the pH and hardness of the water in the aquarium, since these two parameters will have some effect on the species of plants and fish which can be kept under the prevailing local conditions.

Adding the plants and fish

Before adding any plants or fish to the aquarium, it is important to 'age' the new tapwater with a good conditioner, thus making it acceptable for fish and plants. Add a full dose to the tank, and disperse it evenly throughout the water.

Plants are best added a day or so after setting up the tank. A two foot aquarium will require at least 30–40 plants. In the foreground, relatively short plants are required to form a border along the tank floor. As indicated in Chapter 5, there are several small, hardy species of Amazon sword, and several smaller species of *Vallisneria*. For the middle-rear regions of the tank, *Hygrophila* and the larger types of *Vallisneria* are quite well suited, often planted in small clumps. The long leaved varieties of *Vallisneria* and *Sagittaria* look particularly attractive along the back and sides, and a large Amazon sword can make a very attractive centrepiece. A possible planting and decor arrangement is provided in the Figure.

Plants require careful planting. Care should be taken to avoid squashing or breaking long, delicate roots. Such roots are best trimmed before planting, rather than folding and forcing them into the planting medium (see Figure). Lead planting weights are available from most aquarium shops, and these are extremely useful at weighting the plants to sit securely in the gravel bed.

Ideally fish should not be added until about a week after setting up the tank. Unless the local tapwater is very hard and/or alkaline, the following fish will be suitable for a 24 × 12 × 12 (or 15) inch aquarium:

5 yellow barbs
5 neon or 5 cardinal tetras
5 black neon or 5 glowlight tetras
1 pair kribensis
1 pair opaline, golden or pearl gourami
4–5 *Corydoras* catfish
1 sucking loach
2 small angelfish
5 zebra danios or 5 pearl danios

If the local tapwater is very hard and alkaline, it will probably be a good idea to

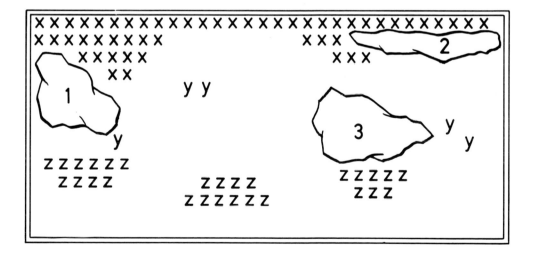

A plan view of a possible tank layout, with rocks (1, 2), cave or piece of bogwood (3), background plants such as **Vallisneria** and **Cabomba** (X), centrepiece or specimen plants such as **Echinodorus** (Y), and foreground plants like dwarf **Vallisneria**, **Echinodorus**, etc (Z).

substitute some of the tetras for livebearing fish such as guppies or mollies. A good community tank of fish in an area of hard, alkaline tapwater is shown below:

5 yellow barbs
2 pairs black mollies
2 pairs guppies
1 pair kribensis
1 pair opaline, golden or dwarf gourami
4–5 *Corydoras* catfish
1 sucking loach
2 small angelfish

All these fish must *not* be added at once. It will take some time for the helpful bacteria in the filter to begin converting waste products from the fish and uneaten food (via the nitrogen cycle) from toxic ammonia through nitrite to less toxic nitrate. Therefore the tank should initially be stocked with a small number of relatively hardy fish (eg yellow barbs), and the characteristic build up and fall of ammonia and nitrite monitored using suitable aquarium test kits.

The levels of ammonia and nitrite in a newly established tank can assume toxic proportions, especially if too many fish are added too soon, or if the tank is overfed. This whole phenomenon is often termed the 'new tank syndrome', and is illustrated in the

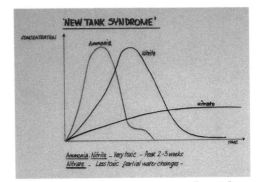

A diagrammatic representation of the water quality changes in a newly established aquarium. Ammonia and nitrite can reach quite high levels during the first two to three weeks, but then usually subside. Since both ammonia and nitrite can be toxic to fish, only small numbers of quite hardy fish should be stocked at this time. Once helpful bacteria become established in the filter, ammonia and nitrite will give way to a gradual increase in nitrate levels. Nitrate is much less toxic, can be used as a food by the aquarium plants, and its level is usually controlled by partial water changes as a part of routine tank maintenance. This 'new tank syndrome' gives a useful insight into the functioning of the tank filters and nitrogen cycle, that were described in Chapter 4.

Figure. To help reduce any toxic effects on the fish that are initially stocked into a new tank, a 25% partial water change can be carried out every few days. Once the ammonia and nitrite levels have fallen and stabilised at a safe level, further fish can be added in small numbers over the ensuing weeks. As a rough guide, allow 10 square inches of water surface for each inch of fish (excluding tail fins). Thus the 24 × 12 inch tank can eventually safely accommodate (288/10) 28 or 29 inches of fish, once the initial settling in period is over. This figure is rather conservative, and experienced hobbyists may be able to keep considerably more fish, especially with good filtration and careful tank management. Such an approach is not recommended for new hobbyists though.

When new fish are obtained they should be quarantined before being added to a set-up tank, to help minimise the introduction of diseases. Some freshwater hobbyists find this procedure unnecessary if they buy their fish from a reliable dealer, but it is then very

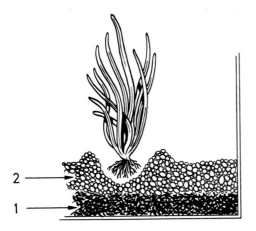

Long trailing roots should be trimmed prior to planting. Note the two layers of substrate on the tank floor, with peat and soil (1) beneath well washed gravel (2).

Allow about 10 square inches of water surface for each inch of fish, but do not add all the fish to a newly established aquarium in one go. Always float new fish in their polythene bag for 15–20 minutes, to let temperatures equalise.

important to keep a close watch for diseases during the week or so following the introduction of the new fish. However, whenever new fish are obtained do not forget to float them in the tank in their polythene carrying bag for 15–20 minutes before releasing them. This will allow water temperatures to equalise and prevent temperature shock.

Tank maintenance

Regular routine aquarium maintenance forms the basis of trouble free fishkeeping, and can be divided into that which must be carried out *daily*, *every two weeks*, and *every month*.

Daily maintenance: this should only take a few minutes each day.

The temperature of the aquarium should be noted at least once a day, which is very simple if there is a reliable thermometer inside (or stuck to the outside of) the aquarium. A variation of one or two degrees is perfectly normal, although wider variations may require investigation. Is the heater-thermostat powerful enough? Is the ther-

mostat functioning properly? Are draughts or room heaters effecting tank temperature?

Unless some form of time switch is installed, the aquarium lights will have to be turned on and off each day, making a note to reduce the amount of lighting if an algal problem begins to develop, or increase the lighting if plant growth is poor. The control of algae is discussed in Chapter 7.

The airpump and the filter it powers must be left on for a minimum 18–20 hours per day. If the pump is turned off for long periods, then detrimental changes may ocur to the helpful bacterial flora of the filter, perhaps adversely affecting aquarium water quality.

Naturally, the fish have to be fed. A community tank of tropical freshwater fish should be fed 2–4 times per day, with only as much food as is consumed in a few minutes. If the fish do not rise eagerly to the surface at each feed, then they may be overfed. Overfeeding must be avoided, since it can result in tank pollution, and even cause the death of the fish. In general, proprietary brands of flaked or tablet foods are superior to homemade, fresh or live foods, because they are of higher quality (being a complete and easily digested, balanced diet), and they may be used with a minimum of fuss and inconvenience, and with no risk of introducing disease organisms. Such prepared foods do, however, provide very concentrated nutrition, which is why they have to be used very sparingly. Live foods can be used to tempt fussy fish, or to bring others into breeding or show condition, although remember that these can introduce pests and diseases.

TANK MAINTENANCE CHECKLIST

Daily

Check temperature
Feed fish
Observe fish

Every two weeks

Measure pH and nitrite content
Remove algae and debris
Partial water change
Filter maintenance
Clean condensation tray
(Thin out plants)
(Rearrange decor)
Check air supply

Every month

Measure water hardness
(Check electrical connections)

Some time each day must be put aside simply for observing the fish. Apart from appreciating their natural grace and beauty, it is also important to watch for any abnormal behaviour or signs of disease.

Every two weeks: the following should be carried out about every two weeks or so.

To begin with, the pH and nitrite content of the aquarium water should be measured using a reliable test kit. As a result of the combined activities of the fish and plants, the pH may vary slightly during the course of a 24 hour period. Also, as already noted, there is a tendency for the pH of the water in a tropical freshwater aquarium to increase towards the alkaline end of the scale with time. Slow drifts (or more sudden jumps) of the pH outside of the usual range for the tank should be watched for and investigated.

The measurement of the nitrite content of aquarium water provides and indication of the degree of organic pollution within a tank, some idea of how the filters are performing and whether the tank is overstocked or the fish overfed. Regular measurements of nitrite content allows action to be taken before a toxic condition develops.

Having measured the pH and nitrite content, the next thing to do is to scrape any algae off the front or side glass of the aquarium with the algae scraper, and the top half inch or so of the gravel should be gently disturbed. After allowing it to settle for a few minutes, the algae and any accumulated debris must then be siphoned out along with about 25% of the water in the tank, preferably using an aquarium gravel washer (such as a *Hydro-clean*). Care must be taken to ensure that gravel or fish are not removed. Regular partial water changes of this kind are very important in correct tank maintenance and in encouraging ideal tank conditions.

With the tank about three-quarters full, it is an excellent opportunity to rearrange any items of tank decor, or perhaps prune back the plants. Before refilling the tank the cartridge from the polyfoam filter should be removed, rinsed in lukewarm water and slipped back onto the filter tube. These cartridges should last very many months without renewal. Do not forget to regularly clean the condensation tray above the tank, since a build up of algae, lime, etc, can significantly reduce the light getting to the plants.

The tank may be refilled using tapwater which has been conditioned and dechlorinated using a good quality conditioner, and brought to approximately the correct temperature using a little boiling water from a kettle. Care should obviously be exercised so that the addition of the water does not disturb too much of the tank decor. If tetras and certain other egglayers are kept, it is also a

A well managed aquarium becomes a beautiful addition to the home, providing hours of fascination. ▶

good idea to add a dose of a 'blackwater tonic' every 7–14 days. This natural blend of peat and plant extracts will have a marked effect on the health, colouration and even breeding of the fish.

Once the air flow to the airstone and filter have been checked, the 'two weekly' maintenance is complete.

Every month: once every month or so (before any partial change is carried out) the hardness of the aquarium water should be measured. Test kits are available which will easily and accurately measure the general hardness (GH) and the carbonate hardness (KH), and the results are usually expressed in ° dH (degrees of German hardness).

As has been mentioned before, the water hardness is related to the amounts of dissolved salts present; in an aquarium the general hardness should not vary very much with time, although (because of plant activity) the carbonate hardness may alter to a greater extent.

Every month or so it is probably a good idea to check the electrical connections of the pump, lights and heater-thermostat, and at rather less frequent intervals (but certainly at least once a year) the fluorescent lighting tubes should be renewed.

39

What about your vacation?

Holiday care is bound to spring to mind as a potential difficulty in setting up an aquarium in the home. The important point to emphasise is that so long as the aquarium is properly maintained for *most* of the time, it can quite easily be left unattended for weekends, and will only require a minimum of attention during longer breaks. The following hints may prove useful.

Weekends: leave filter and airstone running, leave lights off or connect to a time switch. 'Two-weekly' (and if relevant 'monthly') maintenance procedures should be carried out towards the end of the week, and the tank given a quick check over last thing on Friday (before you depart) and first thing on Monday (when you return). Do not feed the fish extra food on Friday (or Monday); they will *not* require feeding over the weekend.

Holidays of up to three weeks duration: leave filter and airstone running, and the lights should be connected to a time switch. Try not to carry out any major tank maintenance a day or two before the holiday. Give the tank a quick check over before departing, and attend to any major maintenance promptly when you return. It is a good idea to get someone to call in to check that no calamity has occurred, once or twice during the holidays. Do not give the fish extra food during the few days before the start of the holiday. Your fish will probably survive quite well without feeding during your absence, but if you wish either get a hobbyist friend to feed your fish every day or so while you are away *or* leave measured quantities of food (in twists of aluminium foil) for a less experienced friend to use. Never forget that non-aquarists are very prone to overfeeding fish, which can have disastrous effects in your absence. Vacation fish food blocks are also available from aquarium shops.

Routine observations of an aquarium are a vital part of successfull fishkeeping.

CHAPTER 7
Creating Special
Water Conditions

The reasons why

Most aquarists can safely rely on their tapwater for fishkeeping, so long as they condition it (to remove chlorine, chloramines, heavy metals and so on) using one of the liquid tapwater treatments that are available from aquarium shops, and bring it to the correct temperature with a little boiling water from a kettle (see Chapter 3).

However, if the hobbyist wishes to keep fish that find the prevailing local tapwater pH and hardness conditions too extreme, or if certain fish require rather special water conditions to thrive and perhaps breed, some thought will have to be given to modification of the chemical characteristics of the tap-water. Here we will examine the production of *soft and acid, hard and alkaline*, and *brackish* water conditions in the home aquarium. Further details on the fish that require these special conditions can be found later in this book. Once again, however, it is emphasised that fish must not be exposed to sudden and drastic changes in water conditions, and hence any modification to aquarium water chemistry is normally carried out under controlled conditions or in the absence of the fish, so that the fish can be gradually accustomed to the changes. Careful use of the water testing kits that are available from aquarium shops is obviously vital to accurately monitor any induced alterations in water chemistry.

Brown, peaty water in nature often indicates soft, acid conditions. When peat is used to help recreate these conditions in the aquarium, ensure that it is aquarium peat and not any other kind, which may contain additional fertilisers and such like.

Soft and acid conditions

The most common requirement is to make tapwater softer and more acid. This can be achieved most easily by allowing water for use in the aquarium to stand in a bucket in contact with aquarium peat for a week or so. Simply tie the peat in a thin nylon bag at a rate of about one handful per gallon of water. Check the pH after 7 to 14 days, when there may have been some reduction in the water hardness too. If after say 3 or 4 weeks the desired pH and hardness has not been reached, it may be necessary to dilute the tapwater with some clean rainwater before allowing it to stand in contact with the peat. A few siting shots will tell you the amount of dilution that is required, and the length of time that the peat must be left in contact. As might be expected, tapwater that is already very hard and alkaline will be more difficult to soften and acidify than tapwater of neutral pH and only medium hardness. However, when making water more soft, it is vital that the KH value is not taken (or subsequently allowed to fall) below about 1° or 2° dH. Below this level the buffering capacity of the KH is easily used up and this can lead to a sudden market shift in pH in the aquarium, with disastrous effects on the fish.

The addition of chemicals to the water (for example citric acid or phosphoric acid) to reduce the pH should be avoided. This is because these chemicals may produce an excess of nutrients in the aquarium which may then cause an algal bloom or cloudy water. Similarly, the addition of strong mineral acids (for example hydrochloric acid) should be avoided since this may cause a drastic reduction in pH and cause a liberation of large amounts of carbon dioxide (which itself, might be dangerous to the fish).

A number of ion-exchange systems have now been developed for aquarium use, which can permit the creation of water with very precise soft, acid conditions. Such systems are available from specialist aquarium shops, but avoid using household water softening devices. Many of these simply exchange 'hard' calcium and magnesium particles for 'soft' sodium particles, leaving the total dissolved salt levels in the water more or less the same. As a result the water may still seem

Discus require soft, acid water to thrive and breed. ▶

'hard' to the fish, or contain high levels of sodium which may cause them further problems.

A number of liquid blackwater 'tonics' or 'extracts' are available from aquarium shops. These add a variety of plant and peat extracts to the water, and impart a slight brown tinge. Although such 'tonics' do not usually effect pH or water hardness, they may add natural constituents that some soft water fish species require to enhance their colouration, condition and encourage spawning.

A word of warning about creating soft, acid conditions. Copper from household water pipes, disease treatments, etc, are more toxic in soft, acid water than hard, alkaline water. Hence special care must be exercised under these conditions. Furthermore, the biological breakdown of ammonia (see Chapter 4) is not favoured by low pH values. Therefore, overfeeding and the accumulation of uneaten food and fish waste is especially dangerous in acid water, and the need for regular partial water changes highlighted. Fortunately, ammonia is much less toxic in acid water than alkaline water. Do note, however, that the toxicity of nitrite is increased in acid water, which is a further reason for ensuring adequate tank and filter maintenance.

The use of clean rainwater has been referred to. Unfortunately rainwater in heavily populated or industrialised areas can be very polluted. However, the levels of these pollutants can be somewhat reduced by collecting rainwater in a continuously overflowing rainwater butt. This helps to dilute out any dissolved pollutants present, since such pollutants are more concentrated in the first minute or two of a rain shower. A piece of nylon netting over the downpipe from a roof will prevent the entry of leaves and other unwanted debris into the rainwater butt.

If you have any doubt about the suitability of local rainwater (or any other water for that matter) for fishkeeping, always use a sample in a test shot involving a few inexpensive fish, before using the water in an established aquarium.

Hard and alkaline conditions

The pH and hardness (GH and KH) of tap-water can be increased quite easily (and slowly) by adding several blocks of limestone to the aquarium, or by using some crushed cockleshell in the tank substrate or in a power filter serving the tank. If desired, the careful use of a strong solution of sodium bicarbonate will increase the pH and KH (but *not* the GH), although this should only be done in the absence of fish and with strong aeration to drive off the liberated carbon dioxide. Various aquarium buffer solutions, rift lake salt mixes and so on are available from aqua-

rium shops. Generally speaking, however, it is best *not* to use marine salts mixer to create hard, alkaline conditions for freshwater fish, as the marine salt mix contains high levels of a range of chemicals (especially sodium) that such fish do not commonly encounter in large amounts in nature. The use of marine salts to create brackish water conditions is referred to below.

As has been mentioned, ammonia is more toxic to fish at an alkaline (high) pH, so a special watch needs to be kept on ammonia levels under such conditions, where biological filtration must be optimal, and overfeeding (and also overstocking) carefully avoided.

Brackish water conditions

Brackish water conditions, as preferred by fish like puffers (*Tetraodon*), finger fish (*Monodactylus*), scats (*Scatophagus*) and some livebearers, can be created most easily using a marine salt mix, along with limestone blocks or cockleshell in the tank. Cooking salt can be used, but avoid table salt which contains some undesirable additives. Many brackish water fish can thrive at a range of salinity values, up to perhaps one quarter or even half strength seawater. Using an aquarium hydrometer designed for use in tropical marine tanks, this corresponds to a specific gravity of around 1.006 to 1.012 in a tropical brackish water tank. Fortunately, many of the fish that prefer brackish water conditions originate from estuaries and mangroves, where salinity values may fluctuate quite dramatically. As a result precise, stable salinity values for these fish are probably not essential in the home aquarium.

When using any kind of dry salt always dissolve it completely (and perhaps aerate for a few hours) before using it for fishkeeping, and remember that oxygen will be less plenti-ful in brackish water, as compared to freshwater, highlighting the need for good aeration in the set-up brackish tank. Similarly, the elevated pH in a brackish water tank (and increased likelihood of ammonia toxicity) emphasises the need for continuous efficient biological filtration to keep this pollutant at an acceptable level. Of course, overfeeding and overstocking must also be prevented.

Maintaining the conditions

Having taken the trouble to create special water conditions in a set-up aquarium, a little time and effort must be spent maintaining them. This means measuring the pH, GH, KH and/or specific gravity as part of the routine tank maintenance, carrying out regular partial water changes, and (of course) using water of the required condition to top-up the tank afterwards.

Note also that when limestone or cockleshell are used in tanks requiring hard, alkaline or brackish water conditions, that their alkaline and hardness enhancing properties will be depleted with time. Thus, occasional part or complete replacement is recommended.

Cichlids from the East African rift lakes like Lake Malawi require a tank with plenty of rocky, refuges and hard, alkaline water.

CHAPTER **8**

Some Common
Pests and Diseases

From time to time a number of pests and fish diseases cause problems in the home aquarium, although almost invariably the onset of the problem can be traced back to some aspect of poor aquarium care or inadequate maintenance. Prevention of such problems is therefore in the hands of the hobbyist.

Pests

Excessive growths of green algae, including green water, are often related to too few plants, too much light and/or overfeeding. An unsightly growth of brown algae often develops under poor lighting conditions. If an algal problem occurs, the first thing to do is to scrape off and siphon out as much of the offending material as possible, using a scraper and a siphon tube. Once the tank has been topped up with water, the recommended dose of a good quality anti-algae treatment should be added to the tank. Next, some attention should be given to preventing further algal problems, and several factors need to be considered.

Even a 24 inch tank will need several dozen plants, in order to utilise the available dissolved nutrients and light that are present in the aquarium. Hence the number of plants may have to be increased in an aquarium which has experienced an algal problem. Furthermore, the duration (and intensity) of the over-tank lighting may have to be decreased, or increased when brown rather than green algae are present.

Excessive amounts of natural sunlight are very good at encouraging green algae too. Finally, you should check to ensure that excessive amounts of fish food are not being

Ramshorn snails like these are probably less of a problem in tropical tanks than some varieties, but their numbers can build up.

added to the tank, as uneaten food can also bring on an algal problem. Do bear in mind that many new tanks go through a short algal bloom and/or experience a short period of 'cloudy water'. If this persists for longer than a week or so, some action should be taken (as described above), checking general tank maintenance as well.

Snails are by no means an essential part of a tropical aquarium, and since some species may develop to pest proportions, it is best to prevent their introduction into a tank if at all possible. A basic preventative measure is to rinse all plants in running water before adding them to a set-up or breeding tank. Snails are unsightly rather than dangerous, but control measures include:

* Introducing fish such as the clown loach and other *Botia* species, opaline gouramis (*Trichogaster trichopterus*), convict cichlids (*Cichlasoma nigrofasciatum*) or puffer fish (*Tetraodon* species) which will feed on some snails.

* Placing one or two fish food tablets on an upturned saucer on the tank floor and leaving it overnight. The snails will be attracted by the tablets and may be removed with a saucer the next morning. You will probably need to tepeat this process every night for a week or so. Do not allow uneaten tablets to pollute the tank.

* Chemical snail eradicators do exist, but be sure to use these carefully, especially in a badly infested tank.

If all else fails, you may need to strip the tank down completely, rinse all the rocks, gravel and decorations in dilute bleach or formalin – followed by a good rinse in clean water – and dip all the plants in a cherry red solution of potassium permanganate or snail eradicator for a few minutes. Note that formalin and blench are very unpleassant chemicals, and are toxic to fish and plants.

Hydra, small freshwater anemone-like creatures, are often introduced into the aquarium with live food. Up to one inch long when extended, their bodies will contract when disturbed, thus masking their characteristic many tentacled appearance. Using the tiny stinging cells in their tentacles, *Hydra* prey on small fish and fish fry in the aquarium. Control measures include:

Fish fungus is easily diagnosed. ▶

* Introducing fish such as gouramis or paradise fish (*Macropodus operculais*) that will prey on *Hydra*.

* Using a six volt battery. Connect two pieces of insulated copper wire to the battery, one to each terminal, and strip the insulation from the other ends of the wire for several centimetres and hang these bare ends of the wire in the tank. Left in the tank for three to six hours, this should bring about the death of most of the *Hydra*, probably by copper poisoning. Immediately afterwards, carry out a 25–50 per cent water change and remove all the dead *Hydra* using a siphon tube. Do not use tapwater conditioners for several days before using this type of treatment.

Flatworms, bristleworms, and one or two other similar invertebrates, are often introduced into the aquarium with live food and they may then thrive in unhygenic, dirty conditions. Uneaten food and accumulated organic matter are a great encouragement to such pests. Rather like snails, these pests are unsightly rather than harmful, although they may attack fish eggs and fry. Control measures include:

* Eliminate overfeeding, increase partial water changes, remove any accumulated debris, wash all plants before introducing them, ensure regular filter maintenance.

* Introduce fish such as gouramis, Siamese fighting fish (*Betta spendens*) or kribensis (*Pelvicachromis pulcher*) to feed on these pests, particularly flatworms.

* Remove all fish and raise the tank temperature to 35° C (95° F) for several hours. This will kill flatworms, although a partial water change and a reduction in temperature will be necessary before the fish can be raintroduced.

If however, all else fails, strip down and refurbish the tank as described for eradicating snails.

It is important to emphasise that the majority of aquarium problems that can occur in the home aquarium can be prevented – simply by setting up the tank correctly to begin with, and then by ensuring regular routine maintenance.

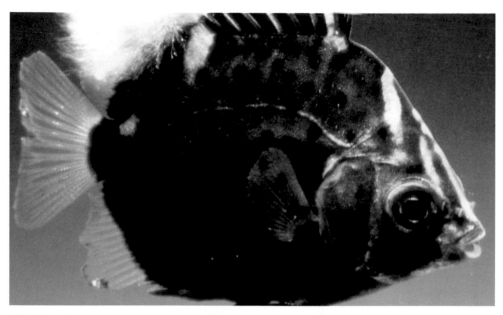

Diseases

White-spot disease is caused by the protozoan parasite *Ichthyophthirius*, which has a direct fish to fish life cycle, and can hence build up quickly within the confines of a well stocked aquarium. It is relatively easy to diagnose, as it appears as small, white pimples about the size of a sugar grain on the skin, fins and gills of fish. Heavily infected fish will scrape against rocks in an irritated fashion, and may suffer from secondary fungal or bacterial infections.

White-spot is usually introduced into an aquarium along with new fish, or perhaps with live foods or plants. Thus quarantining all new fish for two weeks or so, and/or a preventative treatment using a proprietary brand of white-spot remedy, is recommended when new stock is added to a set-up tank. Also, be sure to give all new plants a good rinse in clean water before placing them in an aquarium containing fish. Fortunately, there are a number of safe, effective white-spot treatments available from aquarium stores, and prompt treatment when the first 'spots' appear usually brings the disease under control.

Sliminess of the skin is caused by heavy infestations of tiny parasites such as *Childo-nella*, trichodinids and *Gyrodactylus*, which irritate the skin of the fish host, causing it to scratch against rocks and the aquarium gravel, and to increase mucus production, which gives the skin a slimy, grey appearance. Fortunately, one or two treatments in the aquarium with a proprietary white-spot remedy (or a similar broad spectrum anti-parasite chemical) usually bring the problem under control. Newly imported fish often suffer from this disease. In common with white-spot, the parasites that cause 'sliminess of the skin' can rapidly build up to disease proportions in a heavily stocked tropical aquarium.

Fungus, such as *Saprolegnia* and *Achyla*, is a common disease among aquarium fish, although it usually only attacks fish that are already in poor condition for some other reason. The spores, or 'seeds', that give rise to the fungal infection are extremely common in water, but can only penetrate the skin of a fish that has been damaged by rough handling, fighting, spawning activity, or attack by other parasites.

If left untreated, the off-white or grey, cotton wool like fungal growth can spread rapidly across the body of the fish, eventually killing it.

Consequently, prompt treatment with a

proprietary brand of fungus remedy is essential.

'*Mouth fungus*', which is caused by the bacterium *Flexibacter*, often occurs in recently imported fish, or those kept in unhygenic conditions. Mollies and certain other livebearers seem particularly prone to the disease. If tackled promptly, outbreaks usually respond to treatment with the proprietary anti-bacterial remedies available from aquatic stores. More stubborn cases can usually be successfully treated with antibiotics supplied by a veterinarian.

Fin rot is usually the result of a localised bacterial infection, brought on by fighting or fin nipping, overcrowding, poor diet, or generally unhygenic tank conditions. The fins appear split and ragged any may be streaked with blood or show reddening at the fin bases. As with all diseases, prompt treatments are important, and there are a number of proprietary brands of aquarium antibacterials that are active against fin rot.

Treating against diseases

Most good aquatic stores should stock a range of treatments suitable for controlling the diseases that commonly affect tropical aquarium fish. Be sure to choose a treatment that comes with full instructions for use, together with details of its active ingredients. Follow the instructions closely and remember that filtration over activated carbon and large amounts of organic matter in the tank, will both reduce the effectiveness of most treatments. Above all, remember that prevention is better than cure. Some further hints on disease treatment are given below.

* Calculate the volume of the tank carefully and deduct about 10% to allow for gravel, rocks, etc. (see Chapter 2).

* Always follow the instructions for use of proprietary remedies *very* carefully.

* Always try a remedy out on one or two individuals before treating a whole batch of delicate or expensive fish.

* Never mix remedies unless you know it is safe. A 50–75% water change and filtration over activated carbon for 12–24 hours should remove most active ingredients.

* Do not overcrowd fish during treatment.

* Do not treat fish in galvanised containers.

* If you are in any doubt about the diagnosis and treatment of a disease of your fish, contact a local vet or fish health specialist.

SOME COMMON FISH DISEASES

Symptoms	Disease	Treatment
White-grey cotton wool like growths on skin, fins	Fungus (*Saprolegnia* etc)	Add recommended dose of a proprietary fungus treatment.
White pimples on skin and fins	White-spot (*Ichthyophthirius* parasite)	Add recommended dose of a proprietary white-spot treatment to tank
Fin rot, tail rot	Often a localised bacterial infection	Add recommended dose of aquarium anti-bacterial
Slimly, grey coating to skin, rapid gill movements, scratching against rocks	External parasite infestation	Add recommended dose of anti-parasite treatment
White or off white tufts around mouth	Mouth 'fungus' (*Flexibacter* bacterium)	Add recommended dose of an aquarium anti-bacterial, or use antibiotics from a veterinarian

CHAPTER 9
Breeding

The fact that many of the commonly kept tropical fish will breed in the home aquarium provides an additional and fascinating dimension to the hobby. Aquarium fish can be divided into two broad groups: *egglayers*, where the female (♀) fish usually sheds her eggs into the water where they are fertilised by the male (♂), and *livebearers*, where the male fish mates with and fertilises the female internally, with the female subsequently giving birth to live young. As a general rule, egglayers produce relatively large numbers of eggs, the fry of which require quite small live foods (eg infusorians, newly hatched brine-shrimp) within a few days of becoming free swimming in the tank. By comparison, most livebearers produce relatively small numbers of fully formed young, which will often feed on fine dried foods from birth.

What is also interesting is the degree of brood protection offered by some parent egglayers. Some, like the danios, barbs and tetras scatter their eggs and therefore offer little or no protection to either their eggs or resultant fry. In contrast, many anabantoids build 'bubble nests' where the eggs and young fry are guarded, usually by the male fish. Cichlids display a fascinating array of brood care techniques, ranging from simple guarding of the eggs and fry to actual mouth-brooding (carrying the eggs and fry in their mouth). Naturally, full details an be found in specialist books.

Preparing to breed

Careful choice of potential parent fish (healthy, active, colourful individuals are preferred) should be followed by a conditioning period where they are offered a variety of foods (including some live food). Attention to water conditions can be very important, especially when dealing with some egglayers. The preferred water conditions for a range of commonly kept tropical fish are indicated

This behaviour in kissing gouramis (*Helostoma temmincki*) is probably a sign of aggression between rivals, rather than a sign of affection.

51

later in this book, and soft, slightly acid water can be very important for the successful spawning of fish like many tetras, barbs and some cichlids (eg discus, *Symphysodon* sp.) (see Chapter 7).

For a number of reasons, not least of which is the fact that most eggs and/or fry are likely to be quickly eaten by the fish in a community tank, serious breeding attempts are usually carried out in a separate tank or tanks. Male and female fish can be brought into condition on either side of a tank divider in a single breeding tank, and then introduced by either moving all the fish into one portion of the divided tank with a hand net, or by removing the divider. Many parent fish are prone to eating their own eggs or fry, and hence steps must be taken to prevent this. Removal of the parent fish after spawning or after the young are born is one method, although various livebearer 'traps' are available, where the female can give birth, and where the young can escape from her cannibalistic tendencies. Some fish (eg many cichlids) do, however, make very caring parents.

Since only small numbers of adult fish are usually kept in the breeding tank at any one time, and since the young fry are initially quite small, only very gentle filtration is usually required. A small foam cartridge filter is ideal for a breeding and/or rearing tank. Regular partial water changes, with water of the correct condition, are still important though.

An indication of the methods of development of some fish is provided in the Figure, and information on some of the sexual characteristics of aquarium fish can be found in the Figure in Chapter 10. Here we will briefly consider the breeding habitats of a small number of easy to breed fish.

Guppy (Poecilia reticulata)

This fish is a livebearer and the male has an elongated anal fin that is modified into a sexual organ (= 'gonopodium'), with which he introduces his milt into the female for internal fertilisation. The anal fin of the female is rounded, and she is generally larger though less brightly coloured than the male.

After mating, the 'pregnancy' of the female lasts about three to five weeks, when she can give birth to up to 200 young (although much smaller broods are common). Ensuring that the tank is well planted, perhaps with some floating plants, will afford the fry some protection, although for maximum fry survival, separation of the young fish from the parents (and other adult fish) is recommended.

The young guppies will feed readily on finely powdered dried foods, which should be offered sparingly several times a day.

It is of interest that in many livebearers (including the guppy) the female can store milt from the male fish for quite long periods, and produce several broods from only one mating.

Zebra danio (Brachydanio rerio)

The zebra danio, like many other danios, is a hardy, easy to care for fish. It is also one of the easiest egglayers to breed. Mature male fish (denoted by their slimmer appearance) are separated from the females, and they are both prepared for breeding by feeding a good varied diet for two or three weeks.

Once the female fish are well rounded and obviously full of eggs, both the male and female are introduced to a spawning tank containing about 4 inches of aged water. The pH and hardness is not critical for the breeding of this hardy species, although raising the temperature in the spawning tank to around 28° C or 82° F is a good idea.

To prevent the parent fish eating their own eggs, a layer of marbles or rounded pebbles should be placed on the floor of the spawning tank. The eggs will fall between the marbles or pebbles, out of reach of the parents.

Generally speaking the adult fish are added to the spawning tank with a ratio of three males to two females. They should spawn over the few days following their introduction into the spawning tank, whereupon they should be removed, segregated and perhaps once more prepared for spawning.

The eggs will hatch about 24 hours after being laid, but the young fry will remain amongst the marbles or pebbles for several days. Once they appear and become free swimming, they should be offered meals of infusorians and newly hatched brineshrimp several times a day until they will accept finely powdered dried foods.

DEVELOPMENT OF FISH

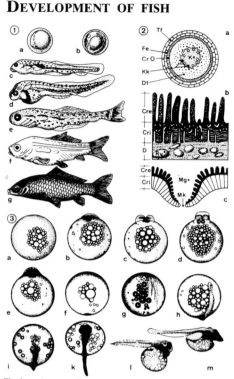

Fig. 1:
The sequence of development in the early life of the goldfish (*Carassius auratius*).
a)–c) Embryonic period: a) Ovular phase; b) Embryonic phase; c) Pre-larval phase;
d) + e) Larval period
f) Juvenile period
g) mature period
h) Ageing period (not illustrated)

Fig. 2:
a) Schematic drawing of a fish egg-cell (oocyte)
b) the egg-cell of an oocyte of the gudgeon (*Gobio gobio*)
c) Micropyle (point through which the sperm passes into the egg)
Cre = cortex radiatus externus, Cri = Cortus radiatus internus, D = yolk, Dt = yolk drops, Fe = epithelial follicle, Mg = micropyle cavity, Mk = micropyle canal, K = nucleus, Kk = nucleotus, Rv = cortical vacuole, Th = Theca folliculi. (The two cortex layers make up the egg case.)

Fig. 3:
Development of *Fundulus heteroclitus*.
a) Egg-cell (oocyte), unfertilized; b) 1-cell stage; c) 2-cell stage d) 4-cell stage; e) 32-cell stage; f) Blastula; g) Gastrula; h) Formation of the eye vesicles; i) First heart movement stage; k) Stage when liver and abdominal cavities are formed; l) Stage when the fin first appear in the tail fin; m) Hatching stage.

PARENTAL CARE IN FISH

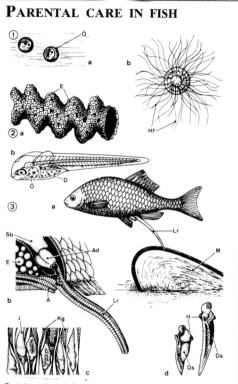

① Adaptation of fish eggs to different ecological conditions.
a) Planktonic eggs: after spawning the eggs float in the upper to middle water levels as a result of the existence of one or several internal oily globules; b) Egg of a substrate-spawning fish. The egg case has formed very fine
Hf = adhesive filaments; O = oily globule.

② a) Section of the spawn thread of a perch (*Perca fluviatis*). The eggs are not laid individually but in strips. The eggs have a thick gelatinous coating that causes them to stick together. These strips of spawn are attached to water plants and the like by the female perch.
b) Five-day old fry of the ruffe (*Gymnocephalus cernua*). The globule of oil and the remaining yolk are still clearly visible.
D = yolk; E = eggs; O = oil

③ a) Bitterling laying eggs in a freshwater mussel. b) Section through the ovary and ovipositor of a female bitterling. c) Position of the bitterling fry between the gill membranes of the freshwater mussel (*Anodonta*). d) Fry of the bitterling at various stages of development. One can clearly make out the attachment pad and the residue of the yolk sac. The attachment pad is a thickening of the head that serves to anchor the embryo fish in the gills of the mussel. Once the fish are ready to hatch, this pad recedes and the 11 mm long fish leave the mussel via the exhalent siphon.
A = anus; Ad = gland; Ds = yolk sac; E = eggs; H = attachment pad; J = young fish; Kg = gill tissue; Lr = ovipositor; M = mussels; Sb = swim bladder.

Since a single female danio can lay several hundred eggs, large broods of fry can result. As the young fish grow, regular partial water changes will have to be instigated and a simple but efficient filter installed (eg foam cartridge filter).

Siamese fighting fish (Betta splendens)

The Siamese fighting fish is now available in a large number of varieties, but they are all relatively easy to keep and also breed. The drab colouration and shorter fins of the female makes sexing quite easy, and mature males are also very aggressive towards other male fighting fish as well as (often) unwilling females. As a result each male is best maintained in isolation in a small tank or large jar, whilst a group of female fighters can be kept together in a small tank.

A ten gallon tank can be set up as the spawning tank, and filled with about 6 inches of aged water at around 27° C or 81° F. Extremes of pH and water hardness should be avoided, and it is a good idea to include a little soft floating vegetation (eg *Cabomba*). Little or no aeration and filtration is required at this stage.

The breeding tank should be divided into two using a clear perforated screen, and a well rounded female placed on one side, and a male fish on the other. Quite quickly the male fish should begin building a nest of bubbles (= 'bubble nest') at the water surface. The female can then be introduced to the male, taking care to watch closely for any overly aggressive behaviour on his part. If the male is showing signs of being too aggressive, the female should be removed, perhaps replacing her with an alternative female. Introduction of mature, egg filled females to a male that has begun bubble nest building eventually brings about the desired result.

After mating, the male collects the eggs in his mouth and spits them into his bubble nest. The eggs are laid in batches throughout the spawning ritual, and broods of several hundred are not uncommon.

After spawning the female is best removed, leaving the male to tend and guard the nest, although after three days it is often a good idea to remove the male too. The eggs hatch after 36–48 hours, but the fry do not become free swimming until day five or six. At this time they require frequent meals of a small live food such as infusorians, but quickly graduate onto fine dried foods and newly hatched brineshrimp.

Since the labyrinth organ of the fighting fish (as well as other anabantoids, like gouramis) begins to develop at three to four weeks of age, the tank must be kept covered to encourage a warm, humid atmosphere above the water surface. Once again, as the fry grow, regular partial water changes and filtration will then become important.

Kribensis or rainbow dwarf cichlid (Pelvicachromis pulcher)

This hardy peaceful fish is ideal for someone who is beginning to become interested in cichlids. It is easy to breed, and will often do so successfully in a community tank. The male fish is larger with more pointed fins than the female, who also has a more rounded appearance and a dark spot at the rear of the dorsal fin. The male has spots on his tail fin.

The kribensis does not appear to have any marked pre-requisites with regard to water quality for spawning, although a good varied diet will help to bring them into spawning condition. A pair will base their territory around a preferred 'cave' in the tank, and defend it against other fish. Onto the inside of the roof of the cave the female will lay about 100 eggs, where they will be fertilised by the male. Both parents usually guard the eggs and the fry (which hatch after three or four days) become free swimming within a week. Newly hatched brineshrimp and finely powdered dried foods are ideal for many cichlid fry, and the young kribensis should be separated from their parents once their shoal begins to break up.

Some suitable fry foods

Aquarium shops can supply a number of liquid and finely powdered dried fry foods. These may be suitable as a first food for relatively large fry such as some livebearers

Siamese Fighting fish (*Betta splendens*) ▶

and cichlids, although many fish (and especially those with very tiny fry, such as anabantoids) benefit from the use of live foods such as infusorians and/or brineshrimp during the first few days after they become free swimming.

Infusorians

Infusorians are tiny single celled animals which may be cultured in large sweet jars. To ensure a continuous supply, a culture needs to be started every 3–4 days, until the fry can take brineshrimp or finely powdered dried foods.

Fill a jar ¾ full with dechlorinated tapwater and add 3 or 4 bruised lettuce leaves or a whole banana skin or even a little hay which has had boiling water poured over it (to break up the cells). Put the jar in a warm, moderately well lit place – with the lid off. Over the ensuing few days the culture should go cloudy (and begin to smell slightly!) and then clear as the infusorians develop. Once the culture is clear and 'sweet smelling', it may be poured into the fry tank – a little at a time. Infusorians are an excellent first food for really small fish fry.

Brineshrimp (Artemia)

Brineshrimp 'eggs' can be obtained from most pet shops, although they are a little expensive. However, the newly hatched schrimps are an excellent food for many small fish fry before the fish can be fed on finely powdered dried foods.

Brineshrimp 'hatcheries' may be bought from most aquatic shops, but the same result may be obtained by using 2–3 clean bottles. Add about two-thirds of a pint of cooled boiled water to one of the bottles and dissolve into this about one heaped teaspoon of cooking salt or marine salts. (A better percentage hatch may be obtained if marine salts are used). Aerate this saltwater and allow to come to room temperature (which should be around 20° C or 68° F). Add enough brineshrimp eggs to cover a 25 cent or two pence coin and place a cotton wool bung in the neck of the bottle. Aerate the saltwater and eggs

continuously and vigorously and the eggs should begin to hatch after about 48 hours. Each 'culture' will then last two or three days, so if you need to maintain a continuous supply of newly hatched brineshrimp over a week or so, you should start off a new culture about every other day.

To remove the newly hatched brineshrimp, simply turn off the aeration and leave the culture to settle for 5–10 minutes. The living brineshrimp will collect about 1–2 inches from the bottom of the bottle, and can be siphoned out, often directly into the fry tank, using a length of airline. To keep the culture going for another day or two, the bottle should be topped up to its previous level with dechlorinated saltwater, and the aeration turned back on.

Always bear in mind that uneaten food will pollute the tank and that fish fry generally require frequent small meals. Always remove uneaten food promptly.

▶

Jewel cichlids (*Hemichromis bimaculatus*) are easy to breed, but very aggressive at spawning time.

CHAPTER **10**

Selecting the Fish

From the 20,000 species of fish that are alive in the world today, several hundred freshwater species are commonly kept by aquarists. This tremendous choice of fish for the home aquarium is one of the reasons why fishkeeping is such a fascinating hobby. However, this very same choice can be a little confusing, especially to the novice fishkeeper.

The correct identification of aquarium fish is obviously of paramount importance. Fortunately the vast majority of the commonly kept tropical fish occur within a handful of well defined families and the information in the Figures should fascilitate some broad taxonomic identifications. Naturally, full colour pictures of a range of popular aquarium species are provided later in this book.

Which fish?

A number of factors will influence any decision regarding the suitability of a particular species for an individual home aquarium. These include the following:

* the size that the fish attain in the aquarium
* its compatibility with other fish, and plants
* the size of the tank that it requires
* its preferred water temperature
* its water chemistry requirements, especially pH and water hardness
* the availability of suitable foods
* the amount of aeration, turbulence and filtration that it requires
* its other environmental and social preferences, since some fish like plenty of free swimming space, while other like rocky or well planted tanks, and some are best kept singly, whilst others should be kept in pairs or shoals.

The importance of most of these factors has been discussed in general terms in earlier Chapters and species specific information will be provided later. Here are outlined a number of the commonly encountered stock selection problems in the tropical freshwater aquarium. It is also important to note, however, that there are always individuals of every species that refuse to conform to the generally accepted 'norm' for that species, especially with regard to anti-social behaviour, predilection for plant destruction and feeding habits. As a result, aquarists must always expect the unusual and be prepared to experiment and, if necessary, modify their approaches to tank care and maintenance.

Water quality requirements

As indicated elsewhere, most of the commonly available tropical aquarium fish will survive over a range of water quality conditions, so long as extreme values and fluctuating water chemistry are avoided. Of particular importance are water temperature, pH and water hardness (see Chapter 3).

When setting up a tank for the first time it is a good idea to measure the pH and water hardness of the local tapwater. If the values are particularly soft and acid, or hard and alkaline, then these characteristics can be modified to more 'middle of the road' values as described in Chapter 7. Alternatively, fish preferring the prevailing local conditions can be kept.

The addition of a small amount of salt to the water can be important when keeping certain popular species, especially mollies (*Poecilia* spp.) This may have an adverse effect on some tropical catfish and tetras in the same tank.

Water chemistry, and the provision of the preferred pH and water hardness values for the species, can be very important for the successful breeding of many egglaying fish (see Chapter 9).

Aggression

A number of popular aquarium species can cause some problems as a result of their occasional aggressive behaviour.

Achieving the correct visual balance of fish is also important. Choose fish that will fill the bottom, middle and upper regions of the tank.

A good example to begin with is the tiger barb (*Barbus tetrazona*). These attractive, active little fish may reach a length of 2–3 inches. They are a hardy, easily kept species, although often labelled as fin nippers. These fish are, like many other barbs, a shoaling species. Hence if you keep a solitary fish or two in a community tank, they may well harass other, especially long finned, fish. However, if you stock the tank with 5 or 6 tiger barbs, you will invariably find that they spend their time harmlessly chasing each other, leaving the other fish alone.

Many of the so called 'sharks' (which are actually members of the same family as the barbs) are rather aggressive to other members of the same species, as well as to other similar looking fish. The red-tailed black shark (*Labeo bicolor*), for example, with its jet black body and striking red tail, is an attractive inmate for any set-up tank. In a community tank a single red-tailed black shark will remain peaceful, even when it reaches its maximum length (of around 4–5 inches). However, if you stock with more than one individual, fights or territorial squabbles may often ensue. Some other sharks can behave in a similar fashion, even towards other fish which just *look* like 'sharks'! The flying fox (*Epalzeorhynchus kallopterus*) and the sucking loach (*Gyrinocheilus aymoneri*) are also that way inclined, and a shark and algae eater living in the same tank may perpetuate quite a running battle, without doing each other any apparent harm. They are probably not to be generally recommended as compatible species for the same community tank though.

Swordtails and platies (*Xiphophorus* spp.) are justifiably very popular aquarium fish. They are hardy, relatively easy to care for and even easy to breed. However, in some instances certain male fish can become dominant in an aquarium and make life very unpleasant for other male platies or swords. The answer is to stock a community tank with only one male – and several females – or ensure that there are plenty of refuges in the tank for the less dominant fish. A Similar problem can occur with some male gouramis (eg dwarf gourami, *Colisa lalia*), who may also harass unwilling females, as well as any reproductive rivals, in the same tank.

Clearly size of the fish, as well as their behavioural tendencies, is very important, and for obvious reasons small neons (*Paracheirodon innesi*) should not be kept with (for example) even medium sized angel fish (*Pterophyllum scalare*).

59

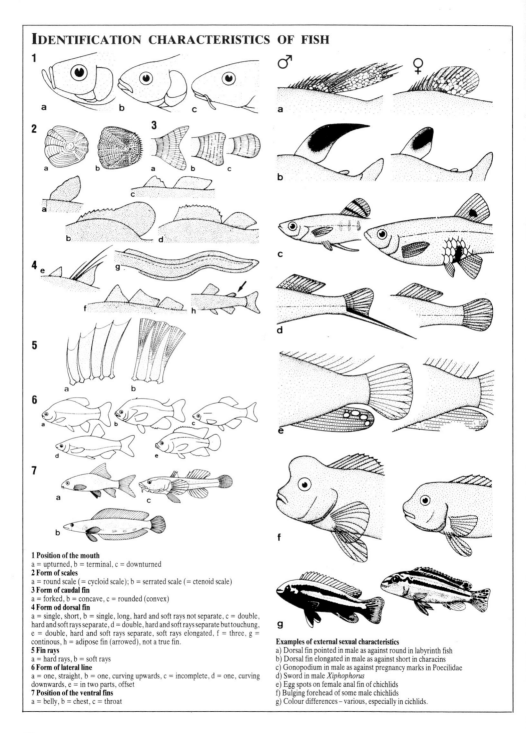

IDENTIFICATION CHARACTERISTICS OF FISH

1 Position of the mouth
a = upturned, b = terminal, c = downturned
2 Form of scales
a = round scale (= cycloid scale); b = serrated scale (= ctenoid scale)
3 Form of caudal fin
a = forked, b = concave, c = rounded (convex)
4 Form od dorsal fin
a = single, short, b = single, long, hard and soft rays not separate, c = double, hard and soft rays separate, d = double, hard and soft rays separate but touchung, e = double, hard and soft rays separate, soft rays elongated, f = three, g = continous, h = adipose fin (arrowed), not a true fin.
5 Fin rays
a = hard rays, b = soft rays
6 Form of lateral line
a = one, straight, b = one, curving upwards, c = incomplete, d = one, curving downwards, e = in two parts, offset
7 Position of the ventral fins
a = belly, b = chest, c = throat

Examples of external sexual characteristics
a) Dorsal fin pointed in male as against round in labyrinth fish
b) Dorsal fin elongated in male as against short in characins
c) Gonopodium in male as against pregnancy marks in Poecilidae
d) Sword in male *Xiphophorus*
e) Egg spots on female anal fin of chichlids
f) Bulging forehead of some male chichlids
g) Colour differences – various, especially in cichlids.

ANATOMY OF A FISH

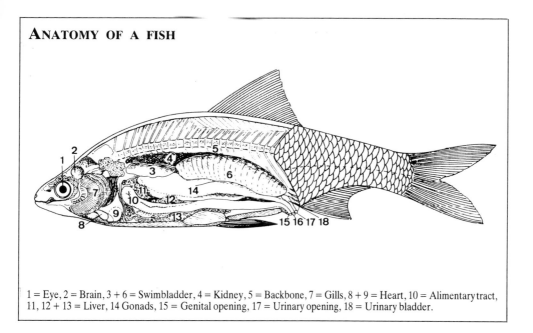

1 = Eye, 2 = Brain, 3 + 6 = Swimbladder, 4 = Kidney, 5 = Backbone, 7 = Gills, 8 + 9 = Heart, 10 = Alimentary tract, 11, 12 + 13 = Liver, 14 Gonads, 15 = Genital opening, 17 = Urinary opening, 18 = Urinary bladder.

MORPHOLOGY OF A FISH

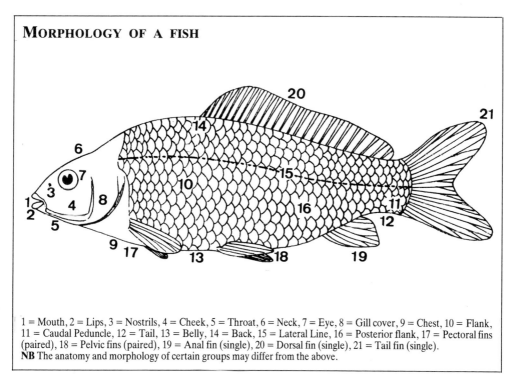

1 = Mouth, 2 = Lips, 3 = Nostrils, 4 = Cheek, 5 = Throat, 6 = Neck, 7 = Eye, 8 = Gill cover, 9 = Chest, 10 = Flank, 11 = Caudal Peduncle, 12 = Tail, 13 = Belly, 14 = Back, 15 = Lateral Line, 16 = Posterior flank, 17 = Pectoral fins (paired), 18 = Pelvic fins (paired), 19 = Anal fin (single), 20 = Dorsal fin (single), 21 = Tail fin (single).
NB The anatomy and morphology of certain groups may differ from the above.

Plants and decor

The provision of a well planted tank with plenty of hiding places can be very useful when mixing species, or mixing numbers of individuals within a species, which would not otherwise be recommended as tank mates. If there are refuges where less dominant or less aggressive fish can hide, or areas of the tank where certain species can set up their territories, then a much more varied (and natural) community will result.

Many beginners are attracted to the cichlids, which is not really surprising when one pauses to consider this varied and often interesting group of fish. However, many of the commonly available species are not really suitable for the community tank. If we look at the popular 'Cichlasoma' genus, we will see that whilst fish like the firemouth cichlid (*C. meeki*) may fit into most tanks when small, as it grows towards its adult size of around 4 inches, it will become considerably more aggressive. At this stage it is really only suitable for a species tank (or for mixing with

other similar sized fish). Similar comments can probably be made about the severum (*C. severum*), the convict cichlid (*C. nigrofasciatum*) and the Jack Dempsey (*C. biocellatum*). By way of contrast, the festive cichlid (*Mesonauta festiva*) can be kept (even as an adult) in most community tanks, although it may uproot plants around its breeding season (which is a common 'Cichlasoma' – trait).

Cichlids for the community tank

Fortunately there are other species of cichlids which can be kept in a community tank, and species within the *Aequidens* genus are particularly unaggressive. These relatively small (often less than 4 inches) South American cichlids are (for the most part) hardy and peaceful. Fish such as the keyhole cichlid (*A. maronii*) and the flag cichlid (*A. curviceps*) will often settle down well in a community set-up, although *A. portalegrensis* and the blue acara (*A. pulcher*) can be more intolerant and destructive (especially at spawning time).

Providing that one or two allowances are made, the kribensis (*Pelvicachromis pulcer*) is perhaps even more ideally suited for a community tank. The tank does need to be at least 24 inches long, well planted and contain a rocky or flower pot cave at either end. A pair of kribensis will then utilise one of these caves for breeding. Other tank mates may occasionally find themselves crowded into the other end of the tank (especially when the cichlid fry become free swimming), but serious problems are usually rare.

(Left) Angelfish can cause problems when kept with small fish like neons, which they can regard as a tasty snack!

Balancing the mix

It is not uncommon for the hobbyist to spend a great deal of time and effort planning the tank layout, its plants, rocks and other decor. Some thought must also be given to achieving the best visual balance of fish in the tank, choosing species which swim in the lower, middle and upper levels. Many catfish and loaches are obvious bottom dwelling species, and fish like most danios and rasboras characteristically swim in the upper regions. Generally the middle regions of the tank should be the most densely populated and tetras, some livebearers and peaceful cichlids are useful in this respect.

The following pages provide a detailed catalogue of around 200 of the most commonly kept aquarium fish. Full colour illustrations are provided for ease of identification, with a comprehensive Index to facilitate location of individual species

Giant gouramis obviously grow too large for the community aquarium and are quite disruptive to plants even when small!

■■■■■■ Suborder Anabantoidei

Suborder Anabantoidei

Group 1: **Suborder Anabantoidei, Labyrinth Fish, Gouramis**

The labyrinth fishes, whose range is limited to Asia and Africa, have as their common characteristic an additional respiratory organ, the so-called labyrinth. These are situated at the side of each gill cavity and are designed to act as back-up organs to supplement the rather inadequate gills in poorly oxygenated water. The fish rise to the surface to obtain additional oxygen from the air. If they are prevented from doing this, then some species may suffocate. As these fish are sensitive to cool external air, their aquarium should be covered.

In some species, the ventral fins have evolved into threads or filaments that act as sensitive, tactile organs containing sensory cells. Most species of labyrinth fish build a nest of bubbles at the surface, usually attached to floating plants but also mixed with fine plant particles. The young and fry are looked after in this bubblenest by the male; the latter alone takes care of the brood until the young are free swimming and start to take food independently.

Breeding them is therefore interesting and not too difficult.

In order to feel at home, almost all labyrinth fish species need plants in the aquarium where they can take refuge from bright light and whenever they are scared. A dark tank bottom is an advantage too. Most species are undemanding when it comes to the type of water and food they require, are well suited to the community tank, and highly recommended for beginners. They are best kept as pairs, though of course several pairs can be kept together, the exception to this being the *Betta* species. However, there should never be a surplus of males.

The species depicted on the following pages from this suborder are classified in the following families or subfamilies.

* *Family* Belontiidae
  Subfamily Macropodinae (Large finned) (M)
  Subfamily Trichogasterinae (Thread Fins) (T)
* *Family* Helostomatidae (Kissing Gouramis) (H)

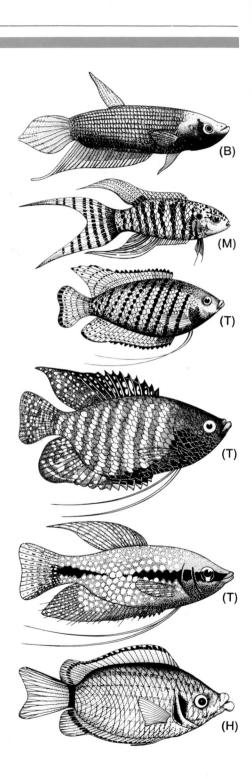

(B)

(M)

(T)

(T)

(T)

(H)

Various body forms of anabantoid fishes

Name	**Fighting fish** (*Betta splendens*)
Distribution range	Indo-China (Malaya, Thailand)
Approx. size (fully grown)	$2^{1}/_{2}$ ins
Sexual differences	The female is much less intensely coloured, no veil-like fins, but with a noticeably bright genital papilla.
Suitability/ difficulty for aquaria	Not difficult but do follow the hints on feeding.
Recommended water conditions	Temperature: 75–86° F; pH: 6.0–8.0; GH: up to 25° dH
Diet	*TetraMin, TetraTips, Tetra FD-Menü, TetraDelica Red Mosquito Larvae.*
Some important pointers	The fancy forms of the Siamese fighting fish come in red, blue, green and other magnificent colour variants. The males need to be kept individually and for this small bowls or jars are adequate. If several of these are lined up next to one another, the full splendour of their colours will be displayed. Two males will fight to the death of kept in a single aquarium. A bubblenest spawner. For community tanks a single male is best, although in larger tanks a pair may be kept.

Name	**Paradise Fish** *(Macropodus opercularis)*
Distribution range	Korea, South China, South Vietnam, Taiwan
Approx. size (fully grown)	4 ins
Sexual differences	The tips of the males' fins are longer and he is more intensely coloured.
Suitability/ difficulty for aquaria	Undemanding, both in terms of water and feeding requirements
Recommended water conditions	Temperature: 68–78° F; pH: 6.0–8.0; GH: up to 30° dH
Diet	*TetraMin, TetraTips,* occasionally small earthworms.
Some important pointers	One of the most beautiful and interesting of all tropical fish. Can be kept in an unheated indoor aquarium. Robust and pugnacious so that it can only be recommended for keeping communally with larger species. Needs a high quality diet. A bubblenest spawner. Low breeding temperature, 76° F or so. Perhaps the first tropical fish to be imported into Europe in the mid 1800's.

Name	**Pygmy or Sparkling Gourami** *(Trichopsis pumilus)*
Distribution range	Viernam, Malaya, Thailand, Sumatra
Approx. size (fully grown)	1¹/₂ ins
Sexual differences	Dorsal and anal fins pointed in male
Suitability/ difficulty for aquaria	Not difficult, but do pay attention to feeding tips below.
Recommended water conditions	Temperature: 75–85° F; pH: 5.8–7.0; GH: 2–10° dH
Diet	*TetraMin, Tetra FD Menu, Artemia* (live)
Some important pointers	A pretty little somewhat timid species. Howewer, because of its shyness and small sise its suitability for the community tank is rather limited. Generally peaceful, but during the breeding season it may become agressive towards other members of the same species. During the courtship display the intensity of its colouration increase quite noticeably. Forms a ball-shaped bubblenest, not usually at the surface but in crevices and under leaves.

Name	**Croaking Gourami** *(Trichopsis vittatus)*
Distribution range	Thailand, Malaya, Borneo, Java, Sumatra
Approx. size (fully grown)	$2^1/_2$ ins
Sexual differences	Tips of fins extended in male
Suitability/ difficulty for aquaria	Needs a lot of attention, both in feeding and general care
Recommended water conditions	Temperature: 75–82° F; pH: 6.5–7.5; GH: 3–15° dH
Diet	*TetraMin, Tetra FD Menu, TetraTips*
Some important pointers	This rather timid natured species is usually rather shy and hence is often last in the pecking order for food in the community tank. It is necessary to devote rather a lot of time to them if they are to be kept healthy over any appreciable period. Both sexes are capable of emitting audible sounds, especially during courtship. Up to 200 eggs laid; a bubblenester.

Name	**Kissing Gourami** *(Helostoma temminckii)*
Distribution range	India, Malaya, Java, Sumatra, Borneo
Approx. size (fully grown)	5 ins (wild specimens much larger)
Sexual differences	In specimens over 4 ins the female is somewhat fuller in shape.
Suitability/ difficulty for aquaria	Not fussy in respect of either water or food
Recommended water conditions	Temperature: 71–82° F; pH: 6.8–8.5; GH: 5–30° dH
Diet	*TetraMin, TetraTips, Tetra Vegetable Flake*
Some important pointers	The readily available semi-albino variety (below) is a domesticated form of the greenish-grey wild form (above). Though the younger ones are well suited for keeping in the living room aquarium, older specimens can become very large. They need warmth but are otherwise undemanding. Any rivalries are settled by means of ritual sparring with the lips being pressed together, hence the name 'kissing' gourami.

Name	**Thick-lipped Gourami** (*Colisa labiosa*)
Distribution range	Indo-China (Burma)
Approx. size (fully grown)	4 ins
Sexual differences	The male is very thick lipped and more intensely coloured than the female
Suitability/ difficulty for aquaria	Not fussy in respect of either water or food
Recommended water conditions	Temperature: 71–82° F; pH: 6.0–7.5; GH: 4–10° dH
Diet	*TetraMin, TetraTips, Tetra Vegetable Flake*
Some important pointers	An easily satisfied, robust species that feels especially at home in well planted tanks with plenty of light. Very suitable for community tanks. Placid nature. Less colourful than the next species. Bubblenest builder, which lays up to 500 or 600 eggs. These hatch after 24 hours, and the fry leave the nest after a further 48 hours.

Name	**Dwarf Gourami** *(Colisa lalia)*
Distribution range	India (Bengal, Assam)
Approx. size (fully grown)	2 ins
Sexual differences	The colouring of the male is markedly more intense
Suitability/ difficulty for aquaria	Not fussy in respect of either water or food
Recommended water conditions	Temperature: 71–82° F; pH: 6.0–7.5; GH: 4–10° dH
Diet	*TetraMin, TetraTips, Tetra Vegetable Flake*
Some important pointers	A magnificently coloured, easy species, seen to best advantage in the company of smaller, placid fish. Likes well illuminated, densely planted tanks with a dark bottom, otherwise it will become rather timid and lose some of its colour. A bubblenest builder that requires plant material to construct its nest. A number of tank-bred strains also exist.

Name	**Honey Gourami** *(Colisa chuna)*
Distribution range	North-east India, Assam
Approx. size (fully grown)	2 ins
Sexual differences	The male is more intensely coloured, particularly during the breeding period
Suitability/ difficulty for aquaria	Not fussy in respect of either water or food
Recommended water conditions	Temperature: 71–82° F; pH: 6.0–7.5; GH: up to 15° dH
Diet	*TetraMin, TetraTips, Tetra Vegetable Flake*
Some important pointers	A very beautiful, tolerant species that is highly suitable for keeping together with small, placid species. They are best kept in pairs in densely planted aquaria. Otherwise as for *Colisa lalia*. Bubblenest builder, which can be territorial at breeding time. Also known as *Colisa sota*.

Name	**Chocolate Gourami** *(Sphaerichthys osphromenoides)*
Distribution range	Sumatra and the Malay Peninsula
Approx. size (fully grown)	2 ins
Sexual differences	Difficult to distinguish. The dorsal fin is rather more pointed in the male.
Suitability/ difficulty for aquaria	Can only be recommended for experienced aquarists because it is rather fussy about the water quality and its food.
Recommended water conditions	Temperature: 77–86° F; pH: 6.0–7.0; GH: 2–4° dH
Diet	*TetraMin, Tetra FD Menu, Artemia* and other live food.
Some important pointers	A highly desirable though, unfortunately, somewhat delicate species. Clean water is a prerequisite if it is to feel ar ease and live any length of time. However, the use of *AquaSafe* makes it possible to keep even this tricky subject. All the same, it is still essential to pay a good deal of attention to its diet – which must include some live food. People have bred them in captivity (they are mouth brooders) and this could prove a gratifying challenge for experienced hobbyists.

Name	**Pearl Gourami** (*Trichogaster leeri*)
Distribution range	Malaya, Thailand, Sumatra, Borneo
Approx. size (fully grown)	4 ins
Sexual differences	The male has an extended dorsal and anal fin and a brick red belly in the breeding season. Slimmer than the female.
Suitability/ difficulty for aquaria	Not fussy in respect of either water or food
Recommended water conditions	Temperature: 73–82° F; pH: 6.5–8.5; GH: 5–50° dH
Diet	*TetraMin, TetraTips, Tetra Vegetable Flake*
Some important pointers	A very beautiful and charming species. Loves roomy, tall, well planted tanks. Cover the surface with floating plants. If it is kept under conditions that are too light it may become rather timid. May be kept in community tanks with smaller species. Pairs form a close bond. Attaches its bubblenest to a leaf.

Name	**Blue or Three-spot Gourami** (*Trichogaster trichopterus*)
Distribution range	Sumatra
Approx. size (fully grown)	3–4 ins
Sexual differences	The male has a highly extended dorsal fin
Suitability/ difficulty for aquaria	Not fussy in respect of either water or food
Recommended water conditions	Temperature: 73–82° F; pH: 6.0–8.8; GH: 5–35° dH
Diet	*TetraMin*
Some important pointers	A widespread, easily cared for species. Not at all fussy about its food or water requirements. Can be kept in the company even of quite small fish. Easy to breed. Very productive; one batch of spawn often producing thousands of young fish. It builds a loose, spreading bubblenest amongst a mass of plants. This species even eats *Hydra* and planarian flatworms. This means that it can be employed as a useful controller of pests in the aquarium. This species occurs in a number of tank bred forms (see below).

Name	**Marbled Gourami** *(Trichogaster trichopterus 'cosby')*
Distribution range	Hybrid form
Approx. size (fully grown)	3–4 ins
Sexual differences	The male has a highly extended dorsal fin and a rather slimmer body.
Suitability/ difficulty for aquaria	Not fussy in respect of either water or food
Recommended water conditions	Temperature: 73–82° F; pH: 6.0–8.8; GH: 5–35° dH
Diet	*TetraMin*
Some important pointers	A favourite hybrid form of the Blue Gourami, hardy and undemanding. Quite peaceable towards other fish generally, though it can often be pugnacious to its own kind. As in the above *Trichogaster trichtopterus* older specimens tend to become rather lazy.

Suborder Characoidei

Group 2: **Suborder Characoidei**
Characins, Tetras

All the species of this suborder hail from South
and Central America and tropical Africa. This
large and extremely diverse suborder encom-
passes approximately 14 families, including the
family Characidae, the genuine American characins in the strictest sense which itself comprises
around 13 subfamilies covering many species
that are suitable for keeping in the aquarium.

Apart from a few exceptions, characoids can be
recognised by their so-called adipose fin, a small
rayless fin, found on the back close to the
caudal fin. Almost all the species are shoaling
fish or at least like to live in groups. They are
seen to their best effect if kept in groups of not
less than four to six per species. It is preferable
to cut down on the number of different species
and keep more of each particular type. Characoids like light aquaria with plants and need
room to swim about. A dark tank bed will help
to show off their generally colourful markings.

Almost all species are free spawners. After a
lively courtship display, the usually numerous
batch of eggs is cast in and amongst fine leaved
plants and their development is then left to
chance. Only a few species practice any form of
brood care.

Characoids need clean, clear, oxygen-rich water
(a properly operating filter will take care of
this). The great majority of these fish can be
kept together with other related species of the
same family, and a variety of other tolerant
community fish.

Generally speaking, characoids are easy to keep
and hence quite suitable for beginners. Apart
from just a few exceptions, they prefer food of
animal origin. They will not scour the bottom of
the tank for food and prefer to take it from the
surface or in mid-water. So a characoid aquarium should be free of floating particles of dirt,
making these fish very suitable for delicate,
contamination sensitive plants.

The species shown on the next few pages are
from the following families.

Anostomidae: Narrow mouthed Characins (A)
Alestidae: African Characins (Al)
Characidae: American Characins (*)
Curimatidae: Headstanders (C)
Gasteropelecidae: Hatchet Fish (G)
Lebiasinidae: Slender Characins or Pencil fish (Le)

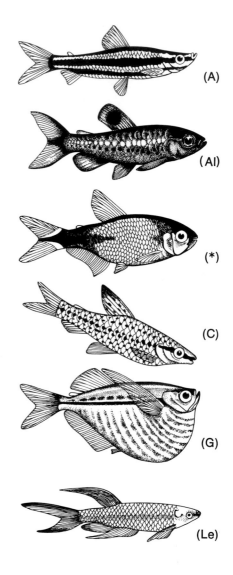

Typical body shapes of characoid fish.

Some authorities have elevated this whole
group of fish to the status of order, under the
heading Characiformes. Nonetheless, the
precise arrangement of the families within the
order or suborder is also still debate.

Name	**Striped Anostomus or Headstander** *(Anostomus anostomus)*
Distribution range	South America (Guyana, Amazonas, Orinoco basin)
Approx. size (fully grown)	5 ins
Sexual differences	Not discernable
Suitability/ difficulty for aquaria	Requires a lot of attention in terms of care and feeding.
Recommended water conditions	Temperature: 71–82° F; pH: 5.8–7.5; GH: up to 20° dH
Diet	*TetraMin, TetraRuby, Tetra FD Menu, TetraTips*
Some important pointers	A charming fish that is peaceable towards other species. Larger specimens are territorial and are pugnacious in defense of their territories and so keeping one specimen is advisable, or alternatively at least three of the same size. Prefers a combination of open swimming space and thickly planted zones. Is seen to best advantage in a decor of narrow, long leaved plants and roots. A suitable subject for community tanks but, being rather timid, loses some of its interest. As yet there are few details available about its reproductive behaviour.

Name	**African Red-eye** *(Arnoldichthys spilopterus)*
Distribution range	Tropical West Africa
Approx. size (fully grown)	3 ins
Sexual differences	The anal fin in the female is only slightly scalloped and does not have any red spots.
Suitability/ difficulty for aquaria	Not fussy in respect of either water or food.
Recommended water conditions	Temperature: 71–82° F; pH: 6.0–7.5; GH: up to 20° dH
Diet	*TetraMin, TetraRuby, Tetra FD Menu*
Some important pointers	A very beautiful and decorative, mobile shoaling fish that really ought to be kept as a shoal. Needs a roomy, well covered aquarium with lots of free swimming space. It loves soft, slightly acid water. Placid natured and easily kept together with fish of a similar size.

Name	**Congo Tetra** *(Phenacogrammus interruptus)*
Distribution range	Congo basin, Africa
Approx. size (fully grown)	$3^{1}/_{2}$ ins
Sexual differences	The tail and the dorsal fin are very elongated in the male though this only becomes apparent when they are 10–12 months old.
Suitability/ difficulty for aquaria	Not difficult but do follow feeding tips.
Recommended water conditions	Temperature: 75–82° F; pH: 6.2; GH: 4–18° dH
Diet	*TetraMin, Tetra FD Menu, Tetra Delica Red Mosquito Larvae*
Some important pointers	An elegant shoaling fish with magnificent fins and colours. It needs a spacious aquarium to cater for its delight in swimming around in open spaces but also plenty of hiding places between plants as well as some protection against bright light under floating vegetation. It takes its food mainly from the surface. Frequent additions of fresh conditioned water are advisable. Also known as *Micralestes interruptus.*

Name	**Spotted Headstander** (*Chilodus punctatus*)
Distribution range	Guayana, Surinam, the whole of the north-east of South America
Approx. size (fully grown)	4 ins
Sexual differences	The female is more powerfully built than the male.
Suitability/ difficulty for aquaria	Requires a lot of attention to its food and care.
Recommended water conditions	Temperature: 75–82° F; pH: 6.0–7.0; GH: up to 10° dH
Diet	*TetraMin, TetraTips, Tetra FD Menu*
Some important pointers	A placid, sociable fish that carries itself with its head tilted sharply downwards (hence its name). Sometimes it can be aggressive towards companions of the same species. Likes dense clumps of plants and hideouts amongst roots. Highly suitable as a subject for the larger community tank.

Name	**Bloodfin** (*Aphyocharax anisitsi*)
Distribution range	Argentina, the river system of the Rio Plata
Approx. size (fully grown)	2 ins
Sexual differences	The male is slimmer
Suitability/ difficulty for aquaria	Not fussy in terms of either water or food
Recommended water conditions	Temperature: 68–78° F; pH: 6.0–8.0; GH: up to 30° dH
Diet	*TetraMin, TetraRuby*
Some important pointers	A cheery little shoaling fish, very tolerant and very well suited for the planted community tank. Lives in the upper water zone. Has no particular requirements but becomes dull and listless if the temperature is too low. Only effective in a shoal. Also known as *Aphyocharax rubripinnis*. Spawns amongst plants and the parents are notorious egg-eaters.

Name	**Black Tetra, Black Widow** *(Gymnocorymbus ternetzi)*
Distribution range	Upper reaches of the Rio Paraguay
Approx. size (fully grown)	2 ins
Sexual differences	The tail lobes of the male are a conspicuous white shade; slimmer than the female.
Suitability/ difficulty for aquaria	Not fussy in terms of either water or food.
Recommended water conditions	Temperature: 71–82° F; pH: 5.8–8.2; GH: up to 30° dH
Diet	*TetraMin*
Some important pointers	An undemanding fish for the beginner. Young, half-grown fish with their deep black fins make a wonderful contrast into the community tank. Very effective and beautiful in a shoal. Has a voracious appetite and, unfortunately, grows too quickly for the adult fish are less striking with grey rather than black fins. The species likes light aquaria with clear water.

Name	**Silver Tip or Copper Tetra** *(Hasemania nana)*
Distribution range	South-eastern Brazil
Approx. size (fully grown)	2 ins
Sexual differences	The male is a shining coppery colour, the female shiny silver and more compact in form.
Suitability/ difficulty for aquaria	Not fussy either in terms of water or food.
Recommended water conditions	Temperature: 71–82° F; pH: 6.0–7.5; GH: 4– 20° dH
Diet	*TetraMin, TetraRuby, Tetra FD Menu*
Some important pointers	This beautifully coloured, lively and peaceable shoaling fish lends itself very well to life in a community tank with similar types of characins like neons – even in small aquaria. It likes a well planted tank, with plenty of free swimming space. Does not have any special requirements but is seen to best advantage against a dark bed and with subdued lighting.

Name	**Red-nosed Tetra** *(Hemigrammus rhodostomus)*
Distribution range	Colombia and the Rio Negro, in black water
Approx. size (fully grown)	2 ins
Sexual differences	The male is somewhat slimmer though they are difficult to tell apart.
Suitability/ difficulty for aquaria	Only recommended for experienced fishkeepers because they have quite specific requirements in respect of food and water quality.
Recommended water conditions	Temperature: 75–82° F; pH: 6.0–7.0; GH: up to 10° dH
Diet	*TetraMin, TetraRuby, Tetra FD Menu, Artemia* (live)
Some important pointers	Peaceable fish that are well suited to a carefully tended aquarium. A lot of attention needs to be paid to their feeding otherwise they are likely to miss out on vital nutrients. It requires a well planted aquarium with plenty of open swimming areas. Provide a soft, slightly acid type of water. Very beautiful species for experienced hobbyists, and it should be kept in a shoal. It is advisable to add *Blackwater Extract / Spawning Aid* at every water change. Similar species, such as *Petitella georgiae* exist too.

Name	**Buenos Aires Tetra** *(Hemigrammus caudovittatus)*
Distribution range	The Rio Plata river system, Argentina
Approx. size (fully grown)	3 ins
Sexual differences	The female is somewhat larger and fuller, fins almost colourless.
Suitability/ difficulty for aquaria	Not fussy in respect of either water or food.
Recommended water conditions	Temperature: 68–78° F; pH: 5.8–8.5; GH: up to 35° dH
Diet	*TetraMin, Tetra Vegetable Flake*
Some important pointers	An undemanding, mobile shoaling fish, very suitable for the beginner and quite easy to breed. Should only be kept in fairly spacious aquaria with plenty of free swimming space. A rather greedy feeder that unfortunately has a penchant for plants, and it is probably for this reason that it is not found in the home aquarium too much these days.

Name	**Glowlight Tetra** *(Hemigrammus erythrozonus)*
Distribution range	North-eastern South America
Approx. size (fully grown)	$1^1/_2$–2 ins
Sexual differences	The male is slimmer, the belly looks flatter.
Suitability/ difficulty for aquaria	Not difficult but do follow the hints on feeding.
Recommended water conditions	Temperature: 75–82° F; pH: 5.8–7.5; GH: up to 15° dH
Diet	*TetraMin, Tetra FD Menu, TetraRuby, Artemia* (live)
Some important pointers	This dainty, very beautiful shoaling fish is seen to best advantage in aquaria with subdued lighting and a dark tank bed (to create the atmosphere of the rain forest). It is only under such conditions that the full beauty of its unique, metallic red lateral stripe running the full length of its body can be appreciated. It needs the same care as the Neon Tetra, and lends itself well to a community tank in the company of these and other small characins.

Name	**Beacon Fish** *(Hemigrammus ocellifer)*
Distribution range	Guyana as far as the Amazonas river system
Approx. size (fully grown)	$1^1/_2$–2 ins
Sexual differences	The male is of slighter build with its swim bladder easily visible against the light, whereas it is partly covered in the female.
Suitability/ difficulty for aquaria	Not difficult but do follow the hints on feeding.
Recommended water conditions	Temperature: 75–82° F; pH: 5.5–7.0; GH: up to 15° dH
Diet	*TetraMin, TetraTips, Artemia* (live)
Some important pointers	A charming, peaceable shoaling fish. The golden iridescent spot located at the root of the tail (hence its name) is really only seen to best advantage in a densely planted aquarium with subdued lighting and a dark bottom. Well suited to the community tank but some care must be given to ensure it gets the proper food.

Name	**Pretty Tetra** *(Hemigrammus pulcher)*
Distribution range	The Peruvian region of the upper Amazon
Approx. size (fully grown)	$1^{1}/_{2}$–2 ins
Sexual differences	The male is rather slimmer and the swim bladder is fully visible against a lighted background.
Suitability/ difficulty for aquaria	Not difficult but do follow the hints on feeding.
Recommended water conditions	Temperature: 75–82° F; pH: 5.5–7.5; GH: up to 15° dH
Diet	*TetraMin, Tetra FD Menu, Artemia* (live)
Some important pointers	A peaceable, somewhat placid shoaling fish, not quite as lively as many of the other characins. Not too shy in a well planted aquarium. Subdued lighting and a dark background brings out the best in the beautiful, metallic bronze sheen of these fish. Unfortunately, this species is not terribly robust and needs peat filtered or similar water.

Name	**Ornate Tetra** *(Hyphessobrycon bentosi bentosi)*
Distribution range	Guyana to the upper reaches of the Amazon
Approx. size (fully grown)	$1^1/_2$–2 ins
Sexual differences	The male has a flag-like extension to its dorsal fin.
Suitability/ difficulty for aquaria	Not fussy in respect of either water or food.
Recommended water conditions	Temperature: 75–82° F; pH: 5.8–7.5; GH: up to 20° dH
Diet	*TetraMin, TetraRuby*
Some important pointers	A very beautiful, attractive and peaceable shoaling fish that lends itself well to keeping with other fish, both smaller and larger. Loves well planted aquaria with shady places where it will occupy the middle to lower water zones. A particularly entertaining feature is the cheerful display of the magnificent males and so at least four to six of them should be kept together. All in all this is one of the most delightful of the characins. Also known as *Hyphessobrycon ornatus*.

Name	**Blood Tetra** (*Hyphessobrycon callistus*)
Distribution range	The Rio Paraguay region
Approx. size (fully grown)	$1^1/_2$ ins
Sexual differences	The male is slimmer and somewhat more intensely coloured.
Suitability/ difficulty for aquaria	Not difficult but do follow the hints on feeding.
Recommended water conditions	Temperature: 75–82° F; pH: 5.8–7.5; GH: up to 25° dH
Diet	*TetraMin, TetraRuby, Tetra FD Menu,* live *Artemia*
Some important pointers	This very beautiful fish with some splendid red tones lives in a loose shoal and is suitable for keeping with other species, provided that these are not too small. If it is short of food it may bite the eyes out of smaller fish on occasion. Needs space in aquarium that is not under-sized and with plenty of plants. Mainly occupies the lower water zones.

Name	**Bleeding Heart Tetra** *(Hyphessobrycon erythrostigma)*
Distribution range	Colombia
Approx. size (fully grown)	2 ins
Sexual differences	In the male the dorsal fin is extended into a long flag-like affair.
Suitability/ difficulty for aquaria	Not difficult but do follow the hints on feeding.
Recommended water conditions	Temperature: 75–82° F; pH: 5.6–7.2; GH: up to 12° dH
Diet	*TetraMin, TetraRuby, TetraTips,* live *Artemia*
Some important pointers	This is a magnificently coloured species. If it is not seen too often in aquaria this may in some measure be due to a lack of availability. Kept on their own, these creatures will pine away. They are best kept with characins of a similar disposition and, say, angelfish. Otherwise as for *Hyphessobrycon bentosi bentosi.*

Name	**Flame Tetra** *(Hyphessobrycon flammeus)*
Distribution range	The area around Rio de Janeiro, Brazil
Approx. size (fully grown)	1$^1/_2$ ins
Sexual differences	In the male the anal fin is a deep red with a velvety black hem, in the female pale pink.
Suitability/ difficulty for aquaria	Not fussy in respect of either water or food.
Recommended water conditions	Temperature: 71–78° F; pH: 5.8–7.8; GH: up to 25° dH
Diet	*TetraMin, TetraRuby*
Some important pointers	One of the oldest of aquarium fish, unfortunately no longer so frequently encountered. Very suitable for the beginner. Peaceable towards one another and towards other species. Fed on *TetraRuby* this fish will develop colouring as intense as under natural conditions. As with many other species in the genus, soft acid ('peaty') water, and fine leaved plants, are important for successful breeding.

Name	**Black Neon Tetra** *(Hyphessobrycon herbertaxelrodi)*
Distribution range	The Amazonas river system
Approx. size (fully grown)	$1^1/_2$ ins
Sexual differences	The male has bluish-white fin tips.
Suitability/ difficulty for aquaria	Not difficult but do follow the hints on feeding.
Recommended water conditions	Temperature: 71–78° F; pH: 5.5–7.5; GH: up to 15° dH
Diet	*TetraMin, Tetra FD Menu*, live *Artemia*
Some important pointers	A charming, peaceable shoaling fish that occupies the upper water zone. It has a most unusual greenish black colouring. A careful watch needs to be kept over this species and care taken over its diet. It is clearly most at ease in situations where the densely planted parts offer plenty of hideaways. A beautiful species for the aquarium specialising in the smaller types of characins.

Name	**Lemon Tetra** *(Hyphessobrycon pulchripinnis)*
Distribution range	South America, the southern tributaries of the Amazon.
Approx. size (fully grown)	$1^1/_2$ ins
Sexual differences	The male is rather slimmer and against a background light the siwm bladder can be seen to be more pointed than in the female.
Suitability/ difficulty for aquaria	Not fussy in respect of either water or food.
Recommended water conditions	Temperature: 75–82° F; pH: 5.5–8.0; GH: up to 25° dH
Diet	*TetraMin, TetraRuby, TetraTips*
Some important pointers	A cheery, peaceable shoaling fish for the well planted aquarium. Seen to best advantage when not in visual competition with other brightly coloured species. This is not the liveliest of species and thrives even in a small aquarium. Only fully grown specimens show the full splendour of their colours, especially if fed on *TetraRuby*.

Name	**Red Phantom Tetra** *(Megalamphodus sweglesi)*
Distribution range	Rio Muco and Rio Meta, and Rio Orinoco, South America
Approx. size (fully grown)	$1^1/_2$ ins
Sexual differences	The male has a dark spot in the middle of the dorsal fin.
Suitability/ difficulty for aquaria	Requires a lot of attention to its feeding and general care.
Recommended water conditions	Temperature: 71–82° F; pH: 5.5–7.5; GH: up to 20° dH
Diet	*TetraMin, TetraRuby, Tetra FD Menu,* live *Artemia*
Some important pointers	The species is arguably even more beautiful than *Hyphessobrycon erythrostigma* and *Hyphessobrycon bentosi bentosi,* and somewhat more demanding regarding its food and water quality. You must be prepared to cater for these whims if you are going to keep them in good health and condition for much more than a year. Best kept with just the smaller characins and dwarf cichlids.

Name	**Red Eyed or Glass Tetra** *(Moenkhausia sanctaefilomenae)*
Distribution range	The river system of the Rio Paraguay, South America
Approx. size (fully grown)	$2^1/_2$ ins
Sexual differences	The male is somewhat smaller and slimmer but they are rather difficult to tell apart.
Suitability/ difficulty for aquaria	Not fussy in respect of either water or food.
Recommended water conditions	Temperature: 68–78° F; pH: 5.5–8.5; GH: up to 30° dH
Diet	*TetraMin*
Some important pointers	An undemanding, peaceable shoaling fish and with its conspicuous red eyes, a very pretty one. Very good for the community tank and also suitable for beginners. It prefers the lower water regions. These fish also love absolutely clear, clean water and dense plant growth with enough swimming room. Not difficult to breed.

Name	**Emperor Tetra** *(Nematobrycon palmeri)*
Distribution range	Colombia
Approx. size (fully grown)	2 ins
Sexual differences	In the male the middle and lower fin rays of the caudal fin are extended, the female is paler.
Suitability/ difficulty for aquaria	Requires a lot of attention to food and care.
Recommended water conditions	Temperature: 71–82° F; pH: 5.0–7.8; GH: up to 25° dH
Diet	*TetraMin, TetraTips, Tetra FD Menu,* live *Artemia*
Some important pointers	A striking shoal fish, well suited to the community tank. Requires frequent, small amounts of food or it may not get enough. The beginner should not attempt to keep this one without making a thorough study of the literature. Adult males are territorial and can be quite frenzied in defence of their own areas.

Name	**Cardinal Tetra** *(Paracheirodon axelrodi)*
Distribution range	The northern tributaries of the Rio Negro
Approx. size (fully grown)	$1^1/_2$ ins
Sexual differences	The male is somewhat more powerfully built but otherwise difficult to distinguish.
Suitability/ difficulty for aquaria	Not too fussy in respect of either water or food.
Recommended water conditions	Temperature: 71–82° F; pH: 5.3–7.8; GH: up to 20° dH
Diet	*TetraMin, TetraRuby, TabiMin, Tetra FD Menu*
Some important pointers	This little gem among fish scarcely lags behind the Neon Tetra in popularity, even though they are often considerably more expensive. Is well suited to the community tank if this is not overstocked and preferably in company with other characins and cichlids, and especially angelfish. This species does require the right kind of care. It likes soft, peat filtered water but will tolerate medium hard water, though it will not develop the full splendour of its colours. A large shoal creates a magical effect in a nicely planted aquarium, especially where a dark bed is also provided. Whereas the breeding of many of the species of characins mentioned here is relatively simple, there are scarcely any fishkeepers – up to and including even the most experienced experts – who have succeeded with the Cardinal Tetra. Practically the entire stock of the many millions of these magnificent fish that populate the aquaria of so many amateurs are taken from the wild. That is to say, they are caught in their native waters in the jungles by professional catchers and are brought in buckets over journeys lasting up to many weeks to the collecting stations of the exporters, usually located in Manaus, whence they are airfreighted to the various importers throughout the world. From here they are distributed by the tropical fish wholesalers to the pet stores where the amateur can purchase them together with a wide range of other species – generally many months after they have been caught. So can it be any surprise that this kind of fish does not come cheap. Captive breeding on fish farms is, however, underway.

Name	**Neon Tetra** *(Paracheirodon innesi)*
Distribution range	The tributaries of the upper course of the Amazon
Approx. size (fully grown)	$1^1/_4$ ins
Sexual differences	Only slight differences, the male being rather slimmer.
Suitability/ difficulty for aquaria	Not fussy in respect of either water or food.
Recommended water conditions	Temperature: 68–78° F; pH: 5.5–8.0; GH: up to 30° dH
Diet	*TetraMin, TabiMin, TetraTips, TetraRuby*
Some important pointers	A peaceable, sociable shoaling fish that shows off its best side when kept in an aquarium of any size with plenty of plants, a dark bed and somewhat subdued lighting. A fairly large shoal kept together with other small characins makes a magnificent sight. Does not come off well with other larger, more greedy types. It is the jewel in the crown amongst fish and certainly number one in the league table of popularity. Does not require especially warm conditions, nor is it demanding in other aspects of its care, though it does need feeding several times a day. One essential prerequisite if it is to do well and live any length of time is clean, nitrite free water. A suitable subject for the amateur. In contrast to the Cardinal Tetra, it is relatively easy to breed this species. A suitable breeding pair would be some young, almost fully grown specimens that one has raised one-self on a good varied diet at a water temperature of around 71° F. First attemps with this breeding pair should take place in a totally clean glass tank about 12 ins long in very soft (about 1–2°) and slightly acidic water (pH around 6) at a temperature of around 75° F. This kind of breeding water can often be produced by filtering mains water over peat. Until the fry are free swimming the breeding tank must be kept in semi darkness as the spawn is light sensitive. During the first stage of their life the young fish require very fine pond plankton and afterwards live *Artemia* and very finely sieved *TetraRuby*. These very brief hints are intended to arouse the interest of the reader only – they do not constitute full breeding instructions. A study of fuller reference works is recommended.

Name	**X-ray Fish** *(Pristella maxillaris)*
Distribution range	Northern South America, tributaries of the Amazon
Approx. size (fully grown)	$1^1/_2$ ins
Sexual differences	The male is slimmer, the translucent, tip of the swim bladder being pointed whereas it is round in the female.
Suitability/ difficulty for aquaria	Not fussy either in terms of water or food.
Recommended water conditions	Temperature: 71–82° F; pH: 6.0–8.0; GH: up to 35° dH
Diet	*TetraMin, TetraRuby*
Some important pointers	A pretty, dainty and undemanding shoal fish that is suitable for the community tank and for the beginner. A very vivacious swimmer and so it should be offered plenty of open space for swimming about as well as lots of plants. Sadly, the species is losing some of its popularity due to the tendency to favour the more colourful fish species. Fed on *TetraRuby*, its fins will develop the red tints of wild caught specimens.

Name	**Penguin Fish** *(Thayeria boehlkei)*
Distribution range	The Amazon river system
Approx. size (fully grown)	2 ins
Sexual differences	In the breeding season the female is rather fuller in form. Otherwise difficult to distinguish.
Suitability/ difficulty for aquaria	Not fussy in respect of either water or food.
Recommended water conditions	Temperature: 71–82° F; pH: 5.8–7.5; GH: up to 20° dH
Diet	*TetraMin, TetraTips*
Some important pointers	A beautiful species and very interesting due to its unique posture when it hangs in the water with its head uppermost. Suitable for the community tank that does not contain too many larger fish and a good subject for the beginner. Not fussy about its food but it is very sensitive to nitrite levels. Likes frequent water changes, using conditioned water. Other species of *Thayeria* Penguin Fish are sometimes available in the trade.

Name	**Marbled Hatchet Fish** *(Carnegiella strigata fasciata)* above *(Carnegiella strigata strigata)* below
Distribution range	Amazonas, Guyana
Approx. size (fully grown)	$1^{1}/_{2}$ ins
Sexual differences	Not discernable
Suitability/ difficulty for aquaria	Requires a lot of attention to feeding and general care.
Recommended water conditions	Temperature: 75–82° F; pH: 5.5–7.5; GH: up to 20° dH
Diet	*TetraMin,, Tetra FD Menu, Tetra Delica Red Mosquito Larvae*
Some important pointers	A peaceable shoaling fish that spends almost all its time just below the surface of the water facing the current. Only suitable for the community tank if kept with other quiet, non aggressive fish. Prone to leaping out of the water! Likes a canopy of floating plants but needs open areas where it can take its food. Unfortunately, rather a delicate subject and not really suitable for beginners. Difficult to breed and little is known about its requirements in this field.

Name	**Silver Hatchet Fish** *(Gasteropelecus sternicla)*
Distribution range	Middle reaches of the Amazon, Guyana
Approx. size (fully grown)	$2^{1}/_{2}$ ins
Sexual differences	Not discernable
Suitability/ difficulty for aquaria	Requires a lot of attention to feeding and general care.
Recommended water conditions	Temperature: 75–82° F; pH: 6.0–7.0; GH: up to 15° dH
Diet	*TetraMin, Tetra FD Menu, Tetra Delica Red Mosquito Larvae*
Some important pointers	A peaceable shoaling fish that likes to stay close to the water surface, where it takes most of its food. Suitable for the community tank and loves to jump (it is the freshwater 'flying fish'), so the aquarium should be well covered. As yet no successful attempts at breeding it are known. Peat filtration advisable as it likes soft water. Otherwise as for *Carnegiella strigata*.

Name	**Splash Tetra** *(Copella arnoldi)*
Distribution range	The Amazon river system and the Rio Para
Approx. size (fully grown)	$2^1/_2$ ins
Sexual differences	The male is more strikingly coloured and all its fins taper out to more of a point.
Suitability/ difficulty for aquaria	Not fussy in respect of either water or food.
Recommended water conditions	Temperature: 75–82° F; pH: 6.5–7.5; GH: 2–12° dH
Diet	*TetraMin, Tetra FD Menu*, live *Artemia*
Some important pointers	An interesting, peaceable fish that is very suitable for the community aquarium, either in a shoal or as a pair. Does not have any special requirements in terms of food or water. A jumper so make sure the tank is totally covered. Prefers to dwell in the upper water zones, just under a cover of floating plants. Spawns above the water surface on overhanging plant leaves or on the covering pane. The male takes charge of brood care, consisting largely of keeping them moist with a spray of water. This species was formerly known as *Copeina arnoldi*.

Name	**Tube-mouthed Pencilfish** *(Nannobrycon eques)*
Distribution range	South America: Amazonas, Guyana
Approx. size (fully grown)	$1^1/_2$ ins
Sexual differences	The ventral fins of the male have bluish-white tips.
Suitability/ difficulty for aquaria	Requires a lot of attention to feeding and general care.
Recommended water conditions	Temperature: 75–82° F; pH: 5.5–7.0; GH: up to 4° dH
Diet	*TetraMin, Tetra FD Menu,* live *Artemia*
Some important pointers	A dainty, delicate fish that does not seem to delight in swimming around too much, preferring to hang around in loose shoals just under the water surface in the shade of floating plants. Not fond of boisterous company. Best kept in the company of characins of the *Nannostomus* genus. Some care has to be paid to the food it is given as it has a very small mouth. It is possible to breed this fish, though it is somewhat difficult.

Name	**Golden Pencilfish** *(Nannostomus beckfordi)*
Distribution range	South America: Amazonas, Guyana, Rio Negro
Approx. size (fully grown)	$1^1/_2$ ins
Sexual differences	The root of the tail is a delicate to blood red in the male while the female has a light red spot in the dorsal fin.
Suitability/ difficulty for aquaria	Not difficult but do follow the hints on feeding.
Recommended water conditions	Temperature: 75–82° F; pH: 6.0–7.5; GH: up to 20° dH
Diet	*TetraMin, TetraRuby, Tetra FD Menu,* live *Artemia*
Some important pointers	A peaceable, pretty shoal fish. At times these fish can display a great deal of liveliness and need lots of swimming room and, at the same time, clumps of fine leaved plants. It is quite possible to breed them in medium-hard water with peat filtration (up to 12° GH and a pH of around 7). Either kept just on their own or with other very small fish, they should breed quite easily.

harrisoni
nitidus

Name	**Dwarf Pencilfish** *(Nannostomus marginatus)*
Distribution range	Surinam
Approx. size (fully grown)	1 ins
Sexual differences	The rear of the male's anal fin is rounded, that of the female pointed.
Suitability/ difficulty for aquaria	Requires a lot of attention to feeding and general care.
Recommended water conditions	Temperature: 75–82° F; pH: 5.8–7.5; GH: up to 15° dH
Diet	*TetraMin, Tetra FD Menu* (crumbled very small), live *Artemia*
Some important pointers	Like the other fish of this group, it lacks an adipose fin. These fish are rather more compact, a good deal smaller and quieter than the slimmer *Nannostomus beckfordi*. It is quite possible to keep a shoal of these delightful, appealing beautifully coloured species in a smallish tank (down to 15 ins), in the company of other very small species if desired. It is possible to breed these, though they are not great producers.

Name	**Three-Banded Pencilfish** *((Nannostomus trifasciatus)*
Distribution range	Middle reaches of the Amazon, Rio Negro, West Guyana
Approx. size (fully grown)	$1^1/_2$ ins
Sexual differences	The female has a slightly rounded belly.
Suitability/ difficulty for aquaria	Requires a lot of attention to feeding and general care.
Recommended water conditions	Temperature: 75–82° F; pH: 5.5–7.0; GH: up to 4° dH
Diet	*TetraMin, Tetra FD Menu, TetraRuby*, live *Artemia*
Some important pointers	General care as for the other pencilfish. Might well be regarded as the most beautiful species in this group. Has a very small adipose fin. Belongs in the specialist aquarium of experienced hobbyists and requires meticulous attention to feeding. More difficult to breed than the other species. **Right: Brazilian habitat of many characins (northern tributary of the Rio Madeira)**

Family Cichlidae

Group 3: **Cichlidae**
The Cichlids

The Cichlids are represented by a large number of species throughout South and Central America (extending into North America) and in Africa, although there are also two species to be found in Asia.

Keeping many species of Cichlid will prove to be equally interesting and pleasurable for beginners and tropical fish experts alike. It is true that many of the larger species of this family will not tolerate other fish or are downright predatory, and others are inveterate 'diggers' and as such only suitable for unplanted specialist aquaria.

But to compensate for this there are amongst the smaller and medium sized species a pleasingly large number of none less desirable species that are well suited to the planted community tank, and which rank alongside the larger species in terms of their very interesting behaviour and brood care. It is largely these species that are recommended in the following pages.

Many species require flowerpots or caves in rock structures as refuges or breeding areas. Many species need to stick their spawn on to some surface, the female laying her eggs usually close together on to a stone or rigid leaf where they are fertilised by the male.

These are then looked after on a fairly intensive basis, either by both parents or by the male or female alone, depending on the species.

A particularly alluring form of behaviour is practised by the mouth brooders, where the spawn, after having been laid and fertilised in a shady hollow, is kept in the mouth of the male, female or both parents, until it matures. What's more, the young fry continue to take refuge and spend the night there for quite some time after hatching.

Furthermore, this family of fish is under much study at the moment, with alternative scientific names proposed for a number of species.

Typical body shapes of Cichlids

Name	**Flag Cichlid** (*Aequidens curviceps*)
Distribution range	The Amazon region
Approx. size (fully grown)	3 ins
Sexual differences	In the male the dorsal and anal fins are longer and more pointed.
Suitability/ difficulty for aquaria	Not fussy in respect of either water or food.
Recommended water conditions	Temperature: 73–82° F; pH: around 7.0; GH: up to 20° dH
Diet	*TetraMin, TetraTips, TabiMin, Tetra Cichlid*
Some important pointers	This pretty species – one of the smallest of the *Aequidens* genus – is also suitable for the community tank because they are not diggers and do not harm plants. Not at all shy and may become so trusting that it will take food from its owner's hand. It has numerous bluish-green dots on its cheeks and fins, giving rise to an alternative common name of Spotted Cichlid.

Name	**Keyhole Cichlid** *(Aequidens maronii)*
Distribution range	Guyana
Approx. size (fully grown)	3¹/₂ ins
Sexual differences	Very slight but the dorsal and anal fins in the male are rather more elongated than in the female.
Suitability/ difficulty for aquaria	Not fussy in respect of either water or food.
Recommended water conditions	Temperature: 71–82° F; pH: 6.0–8.0; GH: up to 20° dH
Diet	*TetraMin, TetraTips, Tetra Cichlid*
Some important pointers	One of the most peaceable and charming of the Cichlids. It is recommended that they are kept in pairs. It is even possible to keep a number of pairs together or in the company of fish of other, smaller species. Does not dig or damage plants. Spawns in shallow, shady hollows and continues to look after its brood for quite a long time, with the youngsters remaining with their parents for months on end.

Name	**Blue Acara** *(Aequidens pulcher)*
Distribution range	South America from the Magdalena river system to Panama
Approx. size (fully grown)	5 ins
Sexual differences	The dorsal and anal fins in older males are extended into a point.
Suitability/ difficulty for aquaria	Not fussy in respect of either water or food.
Recommended water conditions	Temperature: 71–82° F; pH: 6.5–8.0; GH: up to 25° dH
Diet	*TetraTips, TetraMin, Tetra Cichlid, Tetra DoroMin*
Some important pointers	A highly recommended, splendid species, suitable for keeping in pairs or in the company of other largish fish. Not a great digger and so it may be kept in planted aquaria, though it might be a good idea to cover the bed with a layer of good sized gravel chips. Possesses a healthy appetite, and the resultant waste products cause rather rapid contamination of the water so frequent partial water changes are essential. Reaches breeding size at $3^{1}/_{2}$ ins long. Spawns on stones and is painstaking in its care of its brood.

Cichlidae

Name	**Thomas' Cichlid** *(Anomalochromis thomasi)*
Distribution range	Tropical West Africa, Sierra Leone
Approx. size (fully grown)	$2^1/_2$ ins
Sexual differences	Slight – the female is a little smaller
Suitability/ difficulty for aquaria	Not fussy in respect of either water or food.
Recommended water conditions	Temperature: 71–82° F; pH: around 6.5; GH: 7–9° dH
Diet	*TetraMin, TetraTips, Tetra Cichlid*
Some important pointers	This pretty and adaptable species is characterised by its general undemanding nature and the ease with which it breeds. It is peaceable towards other members of its species and other fish. Rock and root structures surrounded by densely planted vegetation will provide refuge in the event of any initial shyness. The young are easily raised, first with live *Artemia* and then with finely crumbled *TetraMin*. This species was known as *Pelmatochromis thomasi*.

Name	**Agassizi's Dwarf Cichlid** (*Apistogramma agassizi*)
Distribution range	The Amazon river system
Approx. size (fully grown)	3 ins
Sexual differences	The female is smaller; the central rays of the caudal fin are extended in the male.
Suitability/ difficulty for aquaria	Requires a lot of attention to feeding and general care.
Recommended water conditions	Temperature: 71–82° F; pH: 6.0–6.5; GH: 5–10° dH
Diet	*TetraMin, TetraTips, Tetra FD Menu, TetraDelica Red Mosquito Larvae,* live food.
Some important pointers	In terms of water quality and food the *Apistogramma* species are significantly more demanding than the previously mentioned *Aequidens* species and the *Cichlasoma* genus dealt with later. Compared with the rest, this species is relatively easy to keep but does need fairly soft, crystal clear water with a low nitrite content – so frequent partial water changes are needed. It prefers to spawn in cavities. The female takes charge of brood care.

Name	**Borelli's Dwarf Cichlid** *(Apistogramma borelli)*
Distribution range	The middle reaches of the Rio Paraguay
Approx. size (fully grown)	3 ins
Sexual differences	The female is smaller, a more intense yellow hue and darker coloured.
Suitability/difficulty for aquaria	Not difficult but do follow the hints on feeding.
Recommended water conditions	Temperature: 71–82° F; pH: 6.0–6.5; GH: 5–10° dH
Diet	*TetraMin, TetraTips, Tetra FD Menu,* live food
Some important pointers	A peaceable and fairly undemanding sort. A good subject for keeping together with other fish. Relatively small tanks will suffice for this species, which displays some very interesting behavioural traits. Prefers to spawn in cavities. One of its features is the variability of its markings.

Name	**Cockatoo Dwarf Cichlid** *(Apistogramma cacatuoides)*
Distribution range	The Amazon basin
Approx. size (fully grown)	$3^1/_2$ ins
Sexual differences	The male is larger than the female. The male's fins are quite markedly extended. These extensions are much shorter in the female. The female turns a yellow colour during the breeding season.
Suitability/ difficulty for aquaria	Requires a lot of attention to feeding and general care.
Recommended water conditions	Temperature: 75–80° F; pH: 6.5–7.2; GH: 4–15° dH
Diet	*Tetra FD Menu, Tetra Delicata Red Mosquito Larvae, TetraRuby*, live food
Some important pointers	This magnificently coloured dwarf cichlid occurs in a variety of colour variants. For breeding purposes a male should be kept with 4–5 females. The eggs are laid in a cavity (for example, a flowerpot). The fry are looked after by several females and raised on live *Artemia*. The species is susceptible to medicines and to water contamination. Use a good water conditioner when adding new water.

Name	**Yellow Regal African Cichlid** *(Aulonocara baenschi)*
Distribution range	Lake Malawi (East Africa)
Approx. size (fully grown)	$4^1/_2$ ins
Sexual differences	The male shows much brighter yellow and blue tones than the grey and brown banded female.
Suitability/ difficulty for aquaria	Not fussy in respect of either water or food.
Recommended water conditions	Temperature: 71–80° F; pH: 7–8.2; GH: 12–30° dH
Diet	*TetraMin, Tetra Cichlid, TetraDelica Red Mosquito Larvae;* young specimens should be given live *Artemia* and *Tetra* fry foods.
Some important pointers	A tank in excess of three feet long is suitable for keeping one pair of these. However, a better solution would be a larger species tank with 2 or 3 cavities as hideouts. Do not keep them together with other species of *Aulonocara,* or some rather undesirable disputes may occur. Fully grown males defend their territories fiercely against their fellows and sometimes do not spare the females. They are quite peaceable towards other species – even smaller ones. To date there are four known colour variants of this species of which the 'Marler' form with the male's orange tail fin, is probably the prettiest.

Name	**Fire-mouth Cichlid** *(Cichlasoma meeki)*
Distribution range	Guatemala, Southern Mexico
Approx. size (fully grown)	5 ins
Sexual differences	The male is more intensely coloured and has longer drawn out dorsal and anal fins.
Suitability/ difficulty for aquaria	Not fussy in respect of either water or food.
Recommended water conditions	Temperature: 71–82° F; pH: around 7.0; GH: up to 10° dH
Diet	*TetraMin, TetraTips, Tetra Cichlid, Tetra DoroMin*
Some important pointers	A bizarre looking, brightly coloured and at the same time undemanding species of Cichlid. Relatively peaceable. Does not dig a great deal and so well rooted, sturdy plants will not suffer too much damage. Brings a bit of variation into the community tank containing medium to large fish. Not difficult to breed. The male is particularly handsome during the breeding season. It keeps at bay anything likely to intrude on the peace of its eggs and fry by a startling display of its raised gill covers. Make sure it has plenty of hiding places in the aquarium. Some authorities refer to this specimen as *Heros* or *Thorichthys meeki*.

Name	**Severum Cichlid** (*Cichlasoma severum*)
Distribution range	Northern Amazon region, Guyana
Approx. size (fully grown)	6 ins
Sexual differences	Fins run out to sharp points in the male which also has conspicuous markings on the head.
Suitability/ difficulty for aquaria	Not fussy in respect of either water or food.
Recommended water conditions	Temperature: 71–82° F; pH: 6.0–6.5; GH: around 5° dH
Diet	*TetraMin, TetraTips, Tetra FD Menu, Tetra Cichlid, Tetra DoroMin*
Some important pointers	A very decorative, undemanding species that used to be very popular. A peaceable sort when young and still outside of the breeding season and hence good for the community tank, even with smaller fish. Because of their similarity in shape to that species, these fish are often nicknamed the 'poor man's discus'. Not especially striking in colour, this fish soon becomes very confiding and will eat out of your hand. Once they reach breeding age, they are best kept on their own in unplanted tanks or otherwise they become aggressive and dig quite a lot. Young fish are often transferred to specially set up hollows and are cared for over a lengthy period. Some authorities now refer to this species as *Heros severus*.

Name	**Golden Julie** *(Julidochromis ornatus)*
Distribution range	Lake Tanganyika
Approx. size (fully grown)	$1^{1}/_{2}$ ins
Sexual differences	Can only be told from the genital papilla in specimens that are ready to mate.
Suitability/ difficulty for aquaria	Only recommended for the experienced hobbyist because of its special requirements in terms of water quality and food.
Recommended water conditions	Temperature: 75–82° F; pH: 8.0–9.0; GH: 11–20° dH
Diet	*TetraMin, TetraTips, Tetra Cichlid*
Some important pointers	There are at least five species of *Julidochromis* that are found in Lake Tanganyika. These species – which do not grow all that large in the aquarium – require caves of a suitable size as a base for forming territorics and breeding. Even if a single pair of them is kept, they should be provided with several cavities where they can take refuge or use as breeding sites. If they are to be kept with other species of African Cichlids, the aquarium should not be less than three feet long, but on their own they can make do with a smaller one. If they are properly kept, they are not difficult to breed successfully.

Name	*Lamprologus brevis*
Distribution range	Lake Tanganyika
Approx. size (fully grown)	$2^{1}/_{2}$ ins
Sexual differences	The male is larger and has an orange coloured edge to its dorsal fin, which is absent in the female. The sex of young specimes is scarcely distinguishable.
Suitability/ difficulty for aquaria	Not difficult but do follow the hints on feeding.
Recommended water conditions	Temperature: 73–78° F; pH: 7.0–8.0; GH: 15–30° dH
Diet	Frozen red mosquito larvae, *Tetra FD Menu,* live *Artemia* and 2 or 3 times a week other live or frozen foods.
Some important pointers	This popular species quickly won the heart of many hobbyists even though it is not all that easy to keep. The aquarium needs to have some areas of open sand where a number of snail shells can be placed. The shells are buried deliberately so that only the opening is visible. Whenever there is a hint of danger these fish will disappear into their 'houses' in a flash. It is here too that they lay their eggs which are looked after by the female – as are the young. These are easily raised on live *Artemia* and *Tetra* fry foods.

Name	*Lamprologus brichardi*
Distribution range	Lake Tanganyika
Approx. size (fully grown)	4 ins
Sexual differences	The fins of the female are not as well developed.
Suitability/ difficulty for aquaria	Not fussy about its water or food.
Recommended water conditions	Temperature: 71–82° F; pH: 7.5–8.5; GH: 10–20° dH
Diet	*TetraMin, TetraTips, Tetra Cichlid, Tetra FD Menu*
Some important pointers	A pretty fish for the beginner and likely to give a great deal of pleasure and encouragement because it breeds quite readily and successfully. It is a cave breeder and practices a similar form of brood care to species of *Julidochromis*, in this case involving both parents, though admittedly not quite as intensive as with some other species. Older males may become rather pugnacious. The aquarium should be set up to include x of varying size. The parent fish leave their older offspring unmolested and simply continue raising their next brood, without driving off the other fry. This is called 'stratified breeding' (i.e. young fish of several age groups grow up in close proximity to one another).

A typical cichlid habitat north of the town of Santa Cruz in Bolivia

Name	**Festive Cichlid** *(Mesonauta festiva)*
Distribution range	The Amazonas river system
Approx. size (fully grown)	$4^{1}/_{2}$ ins
Sexual differences	Outside of the breeding season the sexes are scarcely distinguishable.
Suitability/ difficulty for aquaria	Not fussy in respect of either water or food.
Recommended water conditions	Temperature: 75–82° F; pH: 6.5–7.5; GH: 5–15° dH
Diet	*TetraMin, Tetra Conditioning Food, Tetra FD Menu, Tetra Cichlid*
Some important pointers	This very beautiful and decorative species should be kept in a roomy aquarium with plenty of plants and additional hiding places amongst rocks and roots because these timid fish take fright easily. So they are perhaps best kept with some placid angelfish with which it lives in its natural habitat. Requires high levels of oxygen and sensitive to nitrite and dirty water. Spawns on rocks or rigid plant leaves. This fish is sometimes referred to as *Cichlasoma festivum*. Both partners undertake the task of caring for the spawn and young.

Name	**Golden-eyed Dwarf Cichlid** *(Nannacara anomala)*
Distribution range	West Guyana
Approx. size (fully grown)	$2^1/_2$ ins
Sexual differences	The male is larger and more intensely coloured.
Suitability/ difficulty for aquaria	Not fussy in respect of either water or food.
Recommended water conditions	Temperature: 71–82° F; pH: 6.2–6.5; GH: around 10° dH
Diet	*TetraMin, Tetra FD Menu, TetraDelica Red Mosquito Larvae*
Some important pointers	An undemanding, beautiful and highly recommended dwarf cichlid. Its colouring and markings can change within minutes, depending on its mood. Not a digger and is peaceable in nature. Very suitable for the planted community tank, and an interesting subject for behavioural study. Spawns in cavities (eg flowerpots). The female takes over responsibility for brood care and will even drive much larger fish away from the eggs and young. Not difficult to breed once you have found a compatible pair.

Name	**Butterfly Dwarf Cichlid** *(Papiliochromis ramirezi)*
Distribution range	The western tributaries of the middle reaches of the Orinoco.
Approx. size (fully grown)	2 ins
Sexual differences	The second fin ray of the dorsal fin is very elongated in the male.
Suitability/ difficulty for aquaria	Requires a lot of attention to its feeding and general care.
Recommended water conditions	Temperature: 75–82° F; pH: around 7.0; GH: up to 10° dH
Diet	*TetraMin, TetraTips, Tetra FD Menu,* young ones should be fed live *Artemia*
Some important pointers	Certainly the most beautiful and popular of the Dwarf Cichlids. It will tolerate even quite hard water but is especially sensitive to a shortage of oxygen and to nitrite, and so an extra sized foam filter and frequent filter changes with additions of fresh water are advised. Requires careful feeding. Spawns on rocks and occasionally in sandy hollows. Both partners alternate in brood care duties. This species is sometimes referred to as *Apistogramma* or *Microgeophagus ramirezi.*

Name	**Dwarf Rainbow Cichlid** *(Pelvicachromis pulcher)*
Distribution range	Tropical West Africa, the Niger delta
Approx. size (fully grown)	$3^{1}/_{2}$ ins
Sexual differences	The male is larger and slimmer with the female being more intensely coloured.
Suitability/ difficulty for aquaria	Not fussy in respect of either water or food.
Recommended water conditions	Temperature: 71–82° F; pH: around 6.5; GH: 8–12° dH
Diet	*TetraMin, TetraRuby*
Some important pointers	Peaceable and well suited to the community tank. The aquarium should be well planted and have a good provision of hiding places. Sensitive to water contamination, especially nitrite. Regular partial water changes using *AquaSafe* are advisable. They are not difficult to breed and care for their brood for a period of some weeks. Formerly known as *Pelmatochromis kribensis*.

Name	*Pelvicachromis taeniatus*
Distribution range	The Niger region, West Africa
Approx. size (fully grown)	3 ins
Sexual differences	The female is more intensely coloured.
Suitability/ difficulty for aquaria	Not fussy in respect of either water or food.
Recommended water conditions	Temperature: 71–82° F; pH: 6.2–6.8; GH: 5–10° dH
Diet	*TetraMin*
Some important pointers	A magnificently coloured, delightful species. Undemanding and peaceable. In the smaller type of community tank only one pair should be kept if possible. Feels particularly at ease in planted aquaria with various hideaways. Not difficult to breed though success depends, of course, on finding a compatible pair. A cave spawner. A number of species of *Pelvicachromis* turn up in the trade, and telling them apart can be difficult.

Name	**Dwarf Mouthbrooder** *(Pseudocrenilabrus multicolor)*
Distribution range	East Africa, the Nile
Approx. size (fully grown)	$2^{1}/_{2}$ ins
Sexual differences	The colouring of the female is significantly paler with no red on the anal fin.
Suitability/ difficulty for aquaria	Not fussy in respect of either water or food.
Recommended water conditions	Temperature: 68–78° F; pH: 6.8–8.2; GH: up to 25° dH
Diet	*TetraMin, TetraTips, Tetra Cichlid*
Some important pointers	An interesting species for biological studies. Peaceable and undemanding. Well suited for the community tank. They should be offered a well planted aquarium with plenty of places where they can hide. Breeding pairs should be allowed to choose their partners from a number of young specimens. The male is quite hectic in his pursuit of the female. The female lays her eggs in hollows where they are fertilised by the male. She then gathers these up into her mouth. She then ceases eating until the fry hatch after about ten days. The youngsters continue to seek refuge in their mother's mouth for some weeks to come. Sometimes referred to as *Hemihaplochromis multicolor*.

Nkamba Bay at the southern end of Lake Tanganyika. It is here that Cichlids from the genera Chalinochromis, Eretmodus, Julidochromis, Lamprologus and Tropheus are found

Name	*Lamprologus compressiceps*
Distribution range	Lake Tanganyika
Approx. size (fully grown)	6 ins
Sexual differences	The sexes are difficult to differentiate.
Suitability/ difficulty for aquaria	Not difficult but do follow the hints on feeding.
Recommended water conditions	Temperature: 72–78° F; pH: 7.0–8.0; GH: 10–25° dH
Diet	Young specimens will take flaked food, but older ones should be given frozen food, *TetraTips* and occasionally live food.
Some important pointers	This is a predatory fish and does not belong in a typical community tank. Its compressed shape enables it to pursue its prey into the deepest, narrowest crevices. It takes young fish and crustaceans (shrimps). It is not aggressive towards fish over 2 ins long. A pair needs a cave to breed in. The eggs and later the young are guarded by the female. They do not dig and leave plants alone.

Name	*Lamprologus leleupi longior*
Distribution range	Lake Tanganyika
Approx. size (fully grown)	4 ins
Sexual differences	The male is larger with pointed fins. These are more rounded in the female.
Suitability/ difficulty for aquaria	Not difficult but do follow the hints in feeding.
Recommended water conditions	Temperature: 73–78° F; pH: 7.5–8.5; GH: 15–35° dH
Diet	Frozen or freeze-dried mosquito larvae, *TetraMin* and, from time to time, some live food.
Some important pointers	This very placid species does not dig and does not harm plants. Even so, only the edge of the aquarium should be planted. A more important factor for these fish are a number of piles of stones and some caves. The males establish territories and defend these against other males, as well as any superfluous females. No more than two pairs should be put in a 25 gallon aquarium. The eggs are laid in a cave. After 3 days the fry are transferred to a hollow in front of the cave and guarded by the female. The young should be raised on live *Artemia* and other fine foods such as *Tetra* fry foods. A sub-species of *Lamprologus leleupi* (the lemon cichlid).

Name	**Golden Cichlid** *(Melanochromis auratus)*
Distribution range	Lake Malawi
Approx. size (fully grown)	4 ins
Sexual differences	The belly of the male is a deep shade of black; this is yellow in the female.
Suitability/ difficulty for aquaria	Not fussy in respect of either water or food.
Recommended water conditions	Temperature: 73–82° F; pH: 7.0–8.5; GH: 15–30° dH
Diet	*TetraMin, Tetra Conditioning Food, Tetra Cichlid*
Some important pointers	Like many of the Malawi cichlids, this beautiful species is one for the specialist. A special aquarium should be set up for these fish with rocky structures containing plenty of caves and crevices extending right up to the water line. If this is done it is possible to keep the different species together. All species prefer hard water. A mouthbrooder; the female broods up to two dozen eggs and resultant fry for around 10–14 days.

Name	**Slender Cichlid** *(Pseudotropheus elongatus)*
Distribution range	Lake Malawi
Approx. size (fully grown)	4 ins
Sexual differences	Less distinctive than in the two previous species. The male has the so-called egg-spots on the anal fin.
Suitability/ difficulty for aquaria	Only recommended for experienced aquarists, although it does not have any special requirements in respect of water quality or food.
Recommended water conditions	Temperature: 71–82° F; pH: around 8.8; GH: 10–18° dH
Diet	*TetraMin, TetraTips, Tetra Cichlid*
Some important pointers	This species is termed as being the prime example of a 'matriarchal family' set-up amongst fish. The male only associates with the female for a very short time during the spawning and fertilisation procedure. Once fertilisation has taken place, the male departs and leaves the female to her own devices in matters relating to brood care.

Name	**Zebra Cichlid** *(Pseudotropheus zebra)*
Distribution range	Lake Malawi
Approx. size (fully grown)	4 ins
Sexual differences	See below
Suitability/ difficulty for aquaria	Only recommended for experienced aquarists. Not fussy in respect of either water or food.
Recommended water conditions	Temperature: 71–82° F; pH: 7.5–8.8; GH: 10–18° dH
Diet	*TetraMin, TetraTips, Tetra Cichlid*
Some important pointers	The colouring of this species is extremely variable, which may be due to the existence of a number of races, localised populations or 'morphs'. The males are coloured dark and whitish grey and have on the anal fin up to six orange-yellow egg spots. The females are similar but more grey-blue and often checkered. Even dwarf forms have been imported that become sexually mature at $2^{1}/_{2}$ ins in length, and there are also red-yellow specimens sold under this name. All of them specialise in grazing on algae and other vegetable matter, for which their mouth and teeth have become specially adapted.

Name	**Orange-blue Zebra Cichlid** *(Pseudotropheus 'zebra')*
Distribution range	Lake Malawi
Approx. size (fully grown)	4 ins
Sexual differences	See below
Suitability/ difficulty for aquaria	Not fussy in respect of either water or food.
Recommended water conditions	Temperature: 71–82° F; pH: 7.5–8.5; GH: 10–28° dH
Diet	*TetraMin, TetraTips, Tetra Cichlid*
Some important pointers	This form, which has been called the 'Red Zebra', has not yet been given a definitive scientific classification. The male is usually blue, though it may be red or pink on occasions. The female is red-yellow, occasionally red and black checkered or, very rarely, totally white. The species will continue to breed in the aquarium for many years. Males of the same size will fight and need to be kept apart.

Marbled Angelfish

Name	**Angelfish** *(Pterophyllum scalare)*
Distribution range	The middle reaches of the Amazon, Guyana
Approx. size (fully grown)	Up to 5 ins in length, height up to 8 ins
Sexual differences	Slight. Before and during the act of spawning, the genital papilla of the female is blunter.
Suitability/ difficulty for aquaria	Not fussy in respect of either water or food.
Recommended water conditions	Temperature: 75–82° F; pH: 5.8–7.5; GH: 4– 18° dH
Diet	*TetraMin, Tetra FD Menu,* frozen foods, *Tetra Cichlid*
Some important pointers	One of the most popular of all aquarium fish. The posture and movements of the adults convey a feeling of great majesty. Peaceable and relatively undemanding. A good subject for keeping in a largish, well planted aquarium, together with other placid types of fish. Sensitive to impurities in the water (eg nitrite), which cause the tips of their fins to rot. The female sticks her eggs on to a broad, rigid surface and the male then fertilises them. In order to raise these artificially, the surface can be removed and put into a fully glazed tank with the same water (without sand), providing good aeration at 78–82° F. The clutch may also be left in with the parents, though there is a degree of risk in this because they may, on occasion, eat the eggs. Nowadays there is a whole series of hybrid forms such as the Black Angel, or the Veiled and Smokey Angels (that have very elongated, pendulous fins). Many of these hybrid forms require a higher level of warmth than the original form, and may also be more susceptible to 'old' water and chemicals. These fish are seen to their best advantage in roomy, tall aquaria (over 18 ins high). They should only be kept with the more placid species. A relatively recent addition to the range of hybrid forms is the Marbled Angel, a rather striking and very desirable subject, and another species *P. altum* is occasionally imported.

Angelfish

Veiled Angel

Black Angel

Golden Angel

Name	**African Blockhead** *(Steatocranus casurius)*
Distribution range	Lower reaches of the Congo
Approx. size (fully grown)	$3^1/_2$ ins
Sexual differences	The bump on the forehead is much bigger in the male.
Suitability/ difficulty for aquaria	Not difficult but do follow the hints on feeding.
Recommended water conditions	Temperature: 71–82° F; pH: 6.5–7.0; GH: 15–17° dH
Diet	*TetraMin, Tetra Conditioning Food, TetraTips, Tetra Cichlid*
Some important pointers	A harmless, very bizarre fish that does well in any aquarium provided with plenty of cavities. These blockheads will sit for hours gazing out of their holes, waiting for food. They will then dart out to take a morsel and quickly disappear into the cave with it. Best kept in pairs. A cave breeder. Not difficult to raise in captivity; broods of around 50 are common.

Name	**Discus fish** *(Symphysodon aequifasciata* and *S. discus)*
Distribution range	Discus originate from various areas of the Amazon region, from the Rio Amazonas itself and its various tributaries.
Approx. size (fully grown)	5 ins
Sexual differences	Only discernable during the act of spawning.
Suitability/ difficulty for aquaria	Only to be recommended for the experienced aquarist because they have rather special requirements in respect of water quality and food.
Recommended water conditions	Temperature: 75–86° F; pH: around 6.5; GH: 2–3° dH
Diet	*TetraMin, TetraTips, Tetra FD Menu,* but freeze dried food or live food is also essential.
Some important pointers	The discus fish are rated as the veritable kings of the tropical fish world. They are calm, regal, impressive and desirable fish. Unfortunately, they are only really suitable for experienced fish hobbyists. There are some fundamental prerequisites that have to be fulfilled before you will be able to even keep, let alone breed, discus successfully. These are: a large aquarium, the very best quality and very soft water, a constantly varying diet of live food, enough time to lavish the loving care they need and – often enough – experience gained over a long period of time. Wild caught stock is considerably more susceptible to problems than captive bred stock. Fortunately a significant number of specialists among tropical fish circles have succeeded in breeding large numbers of discus fish and making them available through the trade. This kind of stock often proves quite unproblematical and will thrive on a diet of *Tetra* foods as listed above. If they are to be kept successfully and breed, the aquarium must be fairly large, at least three feet long and 18 ins high and if at all possible, larger still. Hideouts amongst strong plants or bogwood roots or suitably sized plant pots with openings that will allow easy access are required. Similarly, they will require partial covering of the water surface with plant leaves or floating vegetation because they shy away from bright light. The water must be very soft and slightly acidic – especially if attempts are to be made at breeding them (1–3° GH, 6–6.5 pH). Even traces of nitrite are harmful, and a constantly extremely low nitrate content seems to be the key to success both for keeping them and breeding them. The reproductive biology of discus fish is interesting. The youngsters feed during the first week of their life exclusively on a secretion that both parents produce on their skin – if they have the right diet – and that the fry pick at. This is quite unusual amongst fish. Any other approach to breeding/raising them seems doomed to failure. If you want to attempt to breed them, it is best to obtain 4–6 young specimens, giving them the very best conditions until a pair of them form an evident bond. If the tank is large enough, several pairs may be kept. It is scarcely possible to persuade them to form alternative pairs at a later date, it seems.

Blue Discus
(Symphysodon aequifasciata haraldi)

Green Discus
(Symphysodon aequifasciata aequifasciata)

Brown Discus (Symphysodon aequifasciata axelrodi)

Name	*Tropheus duboisi*
Distribution range	Lake Tanganyika – in the deeper areas
Approx. size (fully grown)	$3^1/_2$ ins
Sexual differences	Not known
Suitability/ difficulty for aquaria	Only recommended for experienced aquarists, although it is not fussy about its water or food.
Recommended water conditions	Temperature: 71–78° F; pH: 7.5–8.5; GH: 10–25° dH
Diet	*TetraMin, TetraTips, Tetra Cichlid*
Some important pointers	In contrast to the Blue Zebra *(Pseudotropheus zebra)* from Lake Malawi which is frequently encountered, this species is only found sporadically, and not often at that. They only live in groups as young fish and thereafter alone or in pairs. However, they are not difficult to breed in captivity. The fry, which hatch from the eggs at a length of $^3/_4$ ins, have a large number of white and blue dots on a dark body and look more reminiscent of tropical marine fish than freshwater fish.

Suborder Cyprinoidei

Group 4: **Suborder Cyprinoidei**
Carp-like fish: Barbs, danios and minnows

This group of fish, widely distributed throughout Asia, Africa, Europe and North America, comprises of a large number of beautiful and popular aquarium fish which are almost without exception undemanding and peaceable and so very acceptable for the community tank. Some species are detritus feeders and scour the bottom for food – a task that they perform seemingly untiringly. In doing so, however, a great deal of decomposing matter is thrown up which can have a detrimental effect on any fine leaved plants because this floating matter tends to become deposited on their surface. For those kinds of fish that can be readily identified as scavengers, it is recommended that *Cryptocoryne* and other large leaved, smooth plants are selected. An efficient filter to extract the various floating substances will, however, make it possible to keep these very useful detritus feeders in limited numbers in the community tank – even in cases where feathery plants are kept too.

Many species are darting shoaling fish that live in the upper and middle zones of the water, taking their food either at the surface or possibly preferring to catch it as it descends. These types need room to swim around so the front third of the aquarium should be free of any aquatic plants. Amongst the barbs there are a number of very easy, accommodating subjects that are nonetheless beautifully coloured and marked. They are mostly highly suited to the small aquarium for a beginner.

Almost all of these species are free spawners, shedding their eggs without brood care. In many of them, raising the young fish is quite simple and not beyond a hobbyist with only limited experience.

The species shown on the next few pages belong to the following families:

Cobitidae	Loaches	(C)
Cyprinidae	Carp-like fish	
Gyrinocheilidae	Algae eaters	(G)

Some authorities have elevated this suborder to the status of order, thus placing these families in the order Cypriniformes.

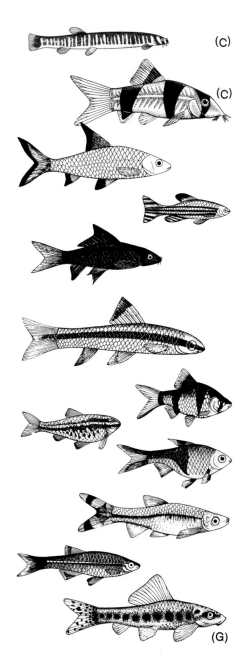

(C)

(C)

(G)

Typical shapes of cyprinid fish: All shapes not accompanied by an alphabetical identification mark belong to the carp-like fish.

Name	**Coolie Loach** *(Acanthophthalmus kuhlii)*
Distribution range	Malaysia
Approx. size (fully grown)	3 ins
Sexual differences	Unknown
Suitability/ difficulty for aquaria	Not fussy in respect of either water or food.
Recommended water conditions	Temperature: 71–82° F; pH: 6–7; GH: up to 20° dH
Diet	*TetraMin, TetraTips, TabiMin*
Some important pointers	Peaceful, gregarious bottom fish. It spends its days hidden away in cavities (such as a flowerpot or half a coconut shell) and its nights assiduously searching for food (as soon as the lights go out, it should be given the appropriate ration of tablet food). It is capable of escaping from the tank via the smallest aperture in the aquarium cover. Well suited to the community tank. A species that will mop up any bits of food left over by other fish but it should not be kept together with the more boisterous types of bottom dwellers.

Name	**Tiger Loach** (*Botia helodes*)
Distribution range	Thailand, Malaya, Singapore, Sunda Islands
Approx. size (fully grown)	4 ins
Sexual differences	Unknown
Suitability/ difficulty for aquaria	Not fussy in respect of either water or food.
Recommended water conditions	Temperature: 71–82° F; pH: 6.0–6.5; GH: up to 5° dH
Diet	*TetraMin, TetraTips, TabiMin*
Some important pointers	A peaceful bottom fish that is territorial and rather pugnacious towards others of the same species. The smaller fish is driven off from any food with crackling sounds that are audible from some metres away. If two different feeding stations are set up then it is possible to keep two or even more specimens in a large tank. It likes to have the opportunity of hiding away amongst dense clumps of plants while at the same time appreciating free swimming room. Hitherto there are no details available on its breeding.

Name	**Red-finned loach** *(Botia lecontei)*
Distribution range	Eastern Thailand, Laos
Approx. size (fully grown)	6 ins
Sexual differences	None recognisable
Suitability/ difficulty for aquaria	Has quite special requirements in terms of water quality, aquarium decoration and food.
Recommended water conditions	Temperature: 75–82° F; pH: 6.0–6.8; GH: 5–15° dH
Diet	*TetraTips, TetraDelica Red Mosquito Larvae, Tetra-Ruby,* once a week it needs live food or deep frozen food.
Some important pointers	These fish require a constant supply of fresh water with a low nitrate content. So it is advisable to change $^1/_4$ to $^1/_3$ of the aquarium water every 7 to 14 days. When doing this, and depending on the quality of the tap-water, it is recommended that *AquaSafe* be added. Loaches like darkened aquaria with plenty of hideouts like clay drainage pipes and so on. The species is very peaceful, with only rival males displaying any aggression. Slightly acidic water is recommended.

Barbs and loaches feeding on TetraTips

Name	**Clown Loach** *(Botia macracantha)*
Distribution range	Sumatra, Borneo
Approx. size (fully grown)	5 ins, in the wild up to 12 ins
Sexual differences	The female is heavier and fatter
Suitability/ difficulty for aquaria	Simple water requirements but do follow the hints on feeding.
Recommended water conditions	Temperature: 75–82° F; pH: 6.0–7.5; GH: 5–20° dH
Diet	*TetraMin, TetraTips, TabiMin*
Some important pointers	A decorative loach that has magnificent markings. It is also very peaceable towards its fellows. Well suited to the community tank and if possible best kept in a smallish shoal when they will stick together for much of the time, making a lively sight. Absolutely essential that they have hiding places amongst rocks and roots. Any breeding successes to date have been purely by chance; it probably spawns in dense clumps of plants.

Name	**Dwarf Loach** *(Botia sidthimunki)*
Distribution range	Thailand
Approx. size (fully grown)	2 ins
Sexual differences	The female is noticeably fuller in the spawning season.
Suitability/ difficulty for aquaria	Simple water requirements but do follow the hints on feeding.
Recommended water conditions	Temperature: 75–82° F; pH: 6.0–7.5; GH: 2–20° dH
Diet	*TetraMin, TetraTips, Tetra FD Menu*
Some important pointers	A dwarfish, very funny, darting and dainty shoaling fish, of the lower water regions. It prefers a fine sandy bed, plenty of plants and needs hiding places. Well suited for the community tank. Nothing known about its breeding to date.

Name	**Silver Shark** *(Balantiocheilus melanopterus)*
Distribution range	Thailand, Sumatra, Borneo
Approx. size (fully grown)	up to 10 ins
Sexual differences	Not discernable
Suitability/ difficulty for aquaria	Not fussy in respect of water or food.
Recommended water conditions	Temperature: 71–82° F; pH: 6.5–7.5; GH: 6–22° dH
Diet	*TetraMin, Tetra Conditioning Food, TetraTips*
Some important pointers	A nimble and very adept swimmer, this species is quite undemanding and robust. Requires large aquaria with long stretches where it can swim freely. For young fish a three foot aquarium is sufficient and in this the fish will cease growing at 4–5 ins in length. As it's a placid type, it is possible to keep it together with smaller species too. Very little is known about its breeding habits under aquarium conditions.

Name	**Rosy Barb** *(Barbus conchonius)*
Distribution range	Northern India, Bengal, Assam
Approx. size (fully grown)	$2^{1}/_{2}$ ins
Sexual differences	The male has reddish brown sides whilst the female's are yellowish.
Suitability/ difficulty for aquaria	Not fussy in respect of either water or food.
Recommended water conditions	Temperature: 64–75° F; pH: 6.5–8.0; GH: 10–30° dH
Diet	*TetraMin, TetraRuby, TetraTips*
Some important pointers	A tough, peaceable and lively shoaling fish that can even be kept together with goldfish in the unheated aquarium. Requires a lot of free swimming room and likes to root around in a soft bed (fine sand). Will nibble at delicate plants. Spawns freely amongst fine leaved plants. Easy to breed. Long finned tank bred varieties are available in the trade.

Name	**Black Ruby Barb** *(Barbus nigrofasciatus)*
Distribution range	Southern Sri Lanka (Ceylon)
Approx. size (fully grown)	2 ins
Sexual differences	The colouring of the male is significantly more intense.
Suitability/ difficulty for aquaria	Not fussy in respect of either water or food.
Recommended water conditions	Temperature: 71–82° F; pH: 6.0–7.5; GH: 12–20° dH
Diet	*TetraMin, TetraRuby, TetraTips, TabiMin*
Some important pointers	A lively peaceful shoaling fish, tough and extremely well suited to a heavily planted community tank. The older males are especially nicely coloured (at their very best when the males outnumber the females). Needs a good deal of swimming room and loves dense background planting. Not difficult to breed.

Name	**Island or Checker Barb** *(Barbus oligolepis)*
Distribution range	Sumatra
Approx. size (fully grown)	$1^1/_2$ ins
Sexual differences	The male has reddish fins with a black edge, the female yellow fins without any edge.
Suitability/ difficulty for aquaria	Not fussy in respect of either water or food.
Recommended water conditions	Temperature: 64–75° F; pH: 6.0–7.5; GH: 10–20° dH
Diet	*TetraMin, TetraTips, TabiMin, TetraRuby*
Some important pointers	The same sort of comments apply as for the species previously described, but it does prefer a soft bed (peat), a more open type of planting and room for free swimming. A delightful little species and even good for the only slightly heated aquarium. Like almost all species of barbs, it prefers clean old water. When the water is changed or fresh water added, *AquaSafe* has a visible 'pick-me-up' effect on its well being. Not difficult to breed.

Name	**Green Barb** *(Barbus semifasciolatus)*
Distribution range	Hong Kong, South eastern China
Approx. size (fully grown)	3 ins
Sexual differences	The female has stronger colouring.
Suitability/ difficulty for aquaria	Not fussy in respect of either water or food.
Recommended water conditions	Temperature: 71–75° F; pH: 6.5–7.8; GH: 10–25° dH
Diet	*TetraMin*
Some important pointers	An easily kept, peaceful fish for any community tank that is not over warm. One of the earliest aquarium fish but only rarely obtainable through the trade these days. This species requires a light, planted aquarium with plenty of hiding places and lots of free swimming room. Easy to breed; up to 300 eggs laid in small batches. These hatch after 36 hours; normal small fry foods are taken.

Name	**Brocade or Schuberti Barb** *(Barbus semifasciolatus 'schuberti')*
Distribution range	A hybrid form
Approx. size (fully grown)	$2^{1}/_{2}$ ins
Sexual differences	The female is a great deal plumper than the male.
Suitability/ difficulty for aquaria	Not fussy in respect of either water or food.
Recommended water conditions	Temperature: 71–82° F; pH: 6.5–8.0; GH: 8–25° dH
Diet	*TetraMin*
Some important pointers	Probably a hybrid form bred from *Barbus semifasciolatus,* the Green Barb. A lively shoaling fish, peaceable and well suited for the community tank. Prefers a copious planting scheme and lots of free swimming room. It enjoys grubbing around on the tank floor and so is likely to cause a hefty coating on delicate plants and therefore it is better if broad leaved plants are used instead. Likes old water. However, if *AquaSafe* is added to the fresh water, it will soon feel just as much at home as in the old water. A free spawner that is not difficult to breed.

Name	**Sumatra or Tiger Barb** *(Barbus tetrazona)*
Distribution range	Borneo, Sumatra, Thailand
Approx. size (fully grown)	2 ins
Sexual differences	At spawning time the female is very heavy and rounded.
Suitability/ difficulty for aquaria	Not fussy in respect of either water or food.
Recommended water conditions	Temperature: 71–82° F; pH: 6.5–7.8; GH: up to 10° dH
Diet	*TetraMin, TetraRuby, TetraTips* and *TabiMin*
Some important pointers	A very popular species of barb – a cheerfully coloured, lively and undemanding shoaling fish. Peaceful, but should not be kept together with angels as they tend to inflict damage on the filaments of the ventral fins of the angelfish. As it gets older it becomes less mobile. It is particularly recommended that the water be changed at regular intervals. An open spawner that is not difficult to breed and raise. A number of tank bred varieties are available, along with a true sub-species, the Banded Barb *(Barbus tetrazona partipentazona)*.

Name	**Two Spot Barb** *(Barbus ticto)*
Distribution range	Malaya, Sumatra
Approx. size (fully grown)	2 ins
Sexual differences	The male is somewhat slimmer and much more highly coloured.
Suitability/ difficulty for aquaria	Not fussy in respect of either water or food.
Recommended water conditions	Temperature: 71–82° F; pH: 6.5–7.8; GH: 10–20° dH
Diet	*TetraMin, TetraRuby*
Some important pointers	A very pretty and lively shoaling fish for the community tank with a stock of vigorous plants around the edges and in the background. It disturbs the bottom substrate less than the Sumatra Barb and does not molest tender plants. Highly recommended. It turns a magnificent ruby red if fed on *TetraRuby*. An open spawner that is easy to breed and rear. *Barbus stoliczkae* is a close relative of this species, and both may be involved in the ancestry of the mysterious 'Odessa' Barb which is now available in the trade.

Name	**Cherry Barb** *(Barbus titteya)*
Distribution range	Sri Lanka (Ceylon)
Approx. size (fully grown)	2 ins
Sexual differences	The male shows a lot of red whereas the female is more yellowish.
Suitability/ difficulty for aquaria	Not fussy in respect of either water or food.
Recommended water conditions	Temperature: 71–82° F; pH: 6.5–7.5; GH: up to 18° dH
Diet	*TetraMin, TetraTips, TetraRuby*
Some important pointers	A peaceable, beautiful though somewhat reticent fish. Prefers to live in the lower water zones. Likes a soft bed and if the plants are growing too thickly is inclined to remain concealed, unfortunately. It is an advantage if they can be seen against some shady floating plants and a dark bed. There is a particularly beautiful red form. In a largish aquarium may be kept in shoals but as pairs in the smaller tank. The males display a degree of rivalry. A free spawner and not difficult to breed. Somewhat rare in its native habitat (Sri Lanka); common in the trade from captive bred sources.

Name	**Pearl Danio** *(Brachydanio albolineatus)*
Distribution range	Northern India, Sumatra, in flowing waters.
Approx. size (fully grown)	2 ins
Sexual differences	The female is heavier and less elegant.
Suitability/ difficulty for aquaria	Not fussy in respect of either water or food.
Recommended water conditions	Temperature: 68–78° F; pH: 6.5–7.0; GH: 5–12° dH
Diet	*TetraMin*
Some important pointers	A peaceful, quite undemanding sort that shimmers like mother of pearl. An indefatigable swimmer that comes over as far too boisterous in a small aquarium. For this reason it can only be recommended to tanks at least three feet long. A keen jumper! Spawns freely in a thicket of plants. Not difficult to breed or raise successfully.

Name	**Leopard Danio** *(Brachydanio frankei)*
Distribution range	See below
Approx. size (fully grown)	2 ins
Sexual differences	The female is more powerfully built and generally lighter.
Suitability/ difficulty for aquaria	Not fussy in respect of either water or food.
Recommended water conditions	Temperature: 68–78° F; pH: 6–8; GH: 4–20° dH
Diet	*TetraMin*
Some important pointers	Probably a captive bred hybrid form that derived from *Brachydanio rerio*. It is a shoaling fish of the middle and upper water zones; peaceful and lively. It is similar to the two previously described, *Brachydanio* species – which are indeed to be preferred to this one. A free spawner and not difficult to breed and raise.

Name	**Spotted Danio** *(Brachydanio nigrofasciatus)*
Distribution range	Upper Burma, in flowing waters
Approx. size (fully grown)	$1^1/_2$ ins
Sexual differences	The belly is orange coloured in the male, slimmer.
Suitability/ difficulty for aquaria	Not fussy in respect of either water or food.
Recommended water conditions	Temperature: 68–78° F; pH: 6.5–7.5; GH: 5–12° dH
Diet	*TetraMin*
Some important pointers	Like the Zebra Danio, this is an ideal fish for the amateur. Perhaps it is rather quieter than the latter, and somewhat smaller. Has only one pair of barbs under the chin. Otherwise like the zebra, which probably surpasses it in popularity because of its very striking stripes. Up to 300 eggs laid in batches; remove parents to prevent cannibalism (as with many Danios). Usual small fry foods will be suitable.

Name	**Zebra Danio** *(Brachydanio rerio)*
Distribution range	The eastern part of the Indian sub-continent, in streams.
Approx. size (fully grown)	$1^1/_2$ ins
Sexual differences	The male is fuller and somewhat brighter than the female.
Suitability/ difficulty for aquaria	Not fussy in respect of either water or food.
Recommended water conditions	Temperature: 68–78° F; pH: 6.5–8.0; GH: 5–25° dH
Diet	*TetraMin, Tetra Conditioning Food*
Some important pointers	With its alluring striped markings, this is one of the most popular and probably most kept tropical fish of all. Hardy and peaceful, it is a lively, skillfull swimmer. Easily cared for and thus particularly well suited for the beginner. Really only seen at its best in a shoal. Easy to breed (see *Brachydanio nigrofasciatus*).

Name	**Giant Danio** *(Danio aequipinnatus)*
Distribution range	Sri Lanka, western part of the Indian sub-continent
Approx. size (fully grown)	5 ins
Sexual differences	The female is plumper and her colouring appears more matt.
Suitability/ difficulty for aquaria	Not fussy in respect of either water or food.
Recommended water conditions	Temperature: 68–78° F; pH: 6.5–7.5; GH: 5–18° dH
Diet	*TetraMin*
Some important pointers	A peaceful shoal fish and a very fast swimmer. It requires a lot of free swimming room in the upper water zones. Quite suitable for the community tank. It grows rather big and larger specimens take on a matt hue and start looking dull. Spawns freely in clumps of plants; not difficult to breed. Also known as *Danio malabaricus.*

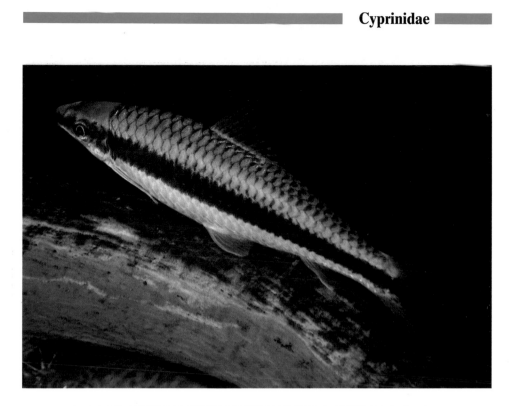

Name	**Siamese Flying Fox** *(Crossocheilius siamensis)*
Distribution range	Thailand, Malaysia
Approx. size (fully grown)	4 ins
Sexual differences	None discernable.
Suitability/ difficulty for aquaria	Not fussy in respect of either water or food.
Recommended water conditions	Temperature: 71–82° F; pH: 6.5–7.8; GH: 5–25° dH
Diet	*Tetra Conditioning Food,* algae, *TetraTips, TetraMin*
Some important pointers	Like the species just described but with rather less conspicuous colouring though a very elegant shape. Peaceful and tolerant towards members of the same species. It is quite the best cleaner up of algae that you can find for the aquarium. If used on a rotation basis, a single specimen can be used to keep a whole series of aquaria free of algae – and will truly thrive on the task! No breeding successes have been heard of. Cover the aquarium because these fish love to leap. Also known as *Epalzeorhynchus siamensis;* other true *Epalzeorhynchus* species are available in the trade (see below).

Name	**Red-tailed Black Shark** *(Epalzeorhynchus bicolor)*
Distribution range	Thailand
Approx. size (fully grown)	5 ins
Sexual differences	None discernable
Suitability/ difficulty for aquaria	Not difficult but do follow the hints on feeding.
Recommended water conditions	Temperature: 75–82° F; pH: around 7.0; GH: up to 15° dH
Diet	*TetraMin, Tetra Conditioning Food, TetraTips, Tetra-Delica Red Mosquito Larvae.*
Some important pointers	Something of a loner, and when just a few are kept is intolerant of members of the same species. However, if four or more of them are kept together in the aquarium, the urge towards territoriality seems to be suppressed. Peaceable towards fish of other species and very well suited to the community tank. Needs lots of hideouts. It likes clean, nitrite free water and regular partial water changes. Given these conditions, it will show very intense colours. Breeding is very difficult and has only succeeded on very odd occasions. Also known as *Labeo bicolor*.

Name	**Red-finned Shark** (*Epalzeorhynchus frenatus*)
Distribution range	South eastern Thailand
Approx. size (fully grown)	6 ins
Sexual differences	Unknown
Suitability/ difficulty for aquaria	Not fussy in respect of either water or food.
Recommended water conditions	Temperature: 71–78° F; pH: 6.5–7.5; GH: 5–25° dH
Diet	*TetraMin, TabiMin*
Some important pointers	A peaceable sort towards all inhabitants of the aquarium, apart from members of the same species, to which it reacts in a cantankerous fashion. For this reason only a single specimen should be kept. Breeding successes in the aquarium have been known, though (apparently) these were quite by chance. It probably spawns in a cavity or crevice. These fish like clear, slightly acidic water and an aquarium that is none too bright. Any plants should be distributed around the edges. Two thirds of the aquarium should be reserved as free swimming room – at least when the fish have reached something approaching their full size. Sometimes referred to as *Labeo frenatus*.

Name	**Flying Fox** (*Epalzeorhynchus kallopterus*)
Distribution range	Sumatra, Borneo
Approx. size (fully grown)	up to 4 ins
Sexual differences	None discernable.
Suitability/ difficulty for aquaria	Not fussy in respect of either water or food.
Recommended water conditions	Temperature: 71–82° F; pH: 6.5–7.5; GH: 5–18° dH
Diet	*TetraMin, Tetra Conditioning Food, TetraTips* and *TabiMin*
Some important pointers	A very placid fish that loves to remain resting on roots and largish plant leaves. A bottom fish that likes to occupy cavities. It is aggressive towards others of the same species in the community tank. Occasionally grazes on algae. Breeding habits not known.

Name	**Red Rasbora, Harlequin Fish** *(Rasbora heteromorpha)*
Distribution range	Malaya, Thailand, eastern Sumatra
Approx. size (fully grown)	$1^1/_2$ ins
Sexual differences	In the female the wedge shaped mark is rounded at the front, in the male it is pointed at the bottom.
Suitability/ difficulty for aquaria	Not fussy in respect of either water or food.
Recommended water conditions	Temperature: 75–82° F; pH: 6.0–7.0; GH: up to 12° dH
Diet	*TetraMin, Tetra FD Menu, TetraRuby*
Some important pointers	A particularly beautiful, very popular shoaling fish of the middle water zone. Also does well as a pair and is well suited to the community tank. It prefers a dark bed and a slightly shaded surface (floating plants). The preferred plants would be species of *Cryptocoryne*. It sticks its eggs to the underside of plant leaves. If peat additives are used when changing the water, this will promote their well being. A similar species, *Heteromorpha hengeli*, is also available.

Name	**Spotted Rasbora** *(Rasbora maculata)*
Distribution range	Malaya, Singapore, Sumatra
Approx. size (fully grown)	1 ins
Sexual differences	The female has a noticeably rounded stomach line.
Suitability/ difficulty for aquaria	Only recommended for experienced aquarists because it has special requirements in terms of water quality and food.
Recommended water conditions	Temperature: 75–82° F; pH: 5.8–6.3; GH: up to 5° dH
Diet	*Tetra FD Menu,* live *Artemia*
Some important pointers	The colours of this delicate little shoaling fish are quite delightful. Only suitable for keeping in association with the very smallest, most placid species (eg *Nannostomus* species, *Corydoras hastatus*). It needs densely planted, fine leaved plants and a dark bed (with a peat coating). A free spawner that is difficult to breed and raise.

Name	**Red-Striped Rasbora** *(Rasbora pauciperforata)*
Distribution range	Sumatra, Malay Peninsula
Approx. size (fully grown)	2 ins
Sexual differences	The female is less slim than the male.
Suitability/ difficulty for aquaria	Not difficult but do follow the hints on feeding.
Recommended water conditions	Temperature: 71–82° F; pH: 5.8–6.5; GH: up to 10° dH
Diet	*TetraMin, Tetra FD Menu*, live *Artemia*
Some important pointers	One of the most elegant of the *Rasbora* species. A peaceful, lively fish which it is essential to keep in a shoal, when it will occupy the middle and upper water zones. It needs a dense planting of fine leaved plants with some free swimming room and a dark bed. Initially somewhat shy. A free spawner and easy to breed.

Name	**Three-line Rasbora, Scissor-tail** *(Rasbora trilineata)*
Distribution range	Malaysia
Approx. size (fully grown)	3 ins
Sexual differences	The female has a curved belly line
Suitability/difficulty for aquaria	Not fussy in respect of either water or food.
Recommended water conditions	Temperature: 71–82° F; pH: 6.0–6.5; GH: up to 12° dH
Diet	*TetraMin, Tetra FD Menu*
Some important pointers	An elegant swimmer and a peaceful sort that is at home in a shoal. Fairly undemanding and very hardy. It inhabits the middle water zone. Dense planting, a dark bed and plenty of free swimming room is desirable. A free spawner that is easy to breed and raise.

Name	**White Cloud Mountain Minnow** *(Tanichthys albonubes)*
Distribution range	China, Hong Kong
Approx. size (fully grown)	$1^1/_2$ ins
Sexual differences	The male is slimmer than the female.
Suitability/ difficulty for aquaria	Not fussy in respect of either water or food.
Recommended water conditions	Temperature: 65–75° F; pH: 6.0–7.8; GH: 5–25° dH
Diet	*TetraMin, TetraRuby, Tetra FD Menu*
Some important pointers	A lively, pretty and very popular shoal fish. It is undemanding and well suited for the beginner. It lives in the middle and upper water zones. Prefers a lot of free swimming room and bright light against a dark bed, otherwise it will not show off its finest colours. A free spawner that is fairly easy to breed and raise. As this species comes originally from moutain streams it is also possible to keep in an unheated aquarium indoors, say with some goldfish.

Name	**Sucking Loach** (*Gyrinocheilus aymonieri*)
Distribution range	Thailand
Approx. size (fully grown)	5 ins
Sexual differences	Unknown
Suitability/ difficulty for aquaria	Not fussy in respect of either water or food.
Recommended water conditions	Temperature: 71–82° F; pH: 6.5–7.5; GH: 5–18° dH
Diet	*TetraMin, TabiMin,* algae
Some important pointers	A peaceable algae-eater that is well suited to the community tank. However, older fishes may from time to time become a nuisance to other large fish by attaching themselves to them with their sucking mouth. Is happy enough with any kind of aquarium decoration provided that it offers enough plants and hiding places. Little is known about its breeding habits.

Barbs and danios in the aquarium

Family Cyprinodontidae

Group 5: **Family Cyprinodontidae**
Egg-laying Tooth Carps, Killifish

The egg-laying tooth carps are found in many regions of America, Africa and Asia and even in Europe.

A significant number of species from this family rank as some of the most colourful of all tropical fish. Unfortunately, however, the care of these little fish is generally not entirely straightforward. They present special problems in respect of the water quality they require, and in terms of feeding, and they can only be kept in the community tank if consideration is given to the specific needs.

The water should be soft and slightly acidic with peat filtration and using peat as material for the tank bed. Regular additions of peat extracts will promote their well being and disease resistance. In the wild many of these species live for only one year – so called seasonal fish – though under aquarium conditions they may survive for a number of years.

They should be given food fairly frequently (at least 4 or 5 times a day), but in smallish portions. It is not really advisable to keep them in conjunction with fish from other families. Nor should the various species be put together without some degree of thought being given beforehand.

These fish are delightful creatures but they could only be recommended for the beginner with some reservations, because their care calls for a degree of experience and a cautious approach. But why not try them in a little aquarium specially set aside for the purpose? But first of all you must acquaint yourself with the details of their special needs by studying the literature that is available through your dealer.

Since *AquaSafe* has been available on the market, the water quality aspect of their care has become more or less unproblematical. Even those species that are regarded as particularly sensitive to water changes, and other disturbances after transport and transfer from one tank to another, will come through their ordeal in good shape if *AquaSafe* is used.

Note that the classification of the Killifish is in a state of revision, with a number of changes proposed.

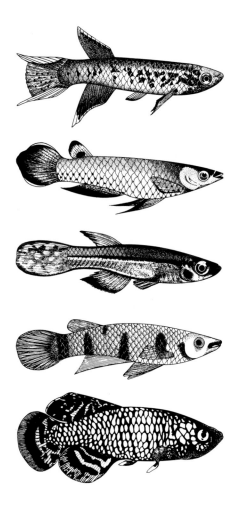

182

Name	**Lyretail** *(Aphyosemion australe)*
Distribution range	West Africa around the Gabon area, in coastal regions
Approx. size (fully grown)	2 ins
Sexual differences	The male is more intensely coloured with porcelain white tips to the fins; the females are plain brown.
Suitability/ difficulty for aquaria	Requires a lot of attention to its general care and feeding.
Recommended water conditions	Temperature: 68–78° F; pH: 5.5–6.5; GH: up to 10° dH
Diet	*TetraMin, TetraTips, Tetra FD Menu,* live *Artemia*
Some important pointers	Quite one of the most beautiful of all tropical fish. Of all the *Aphyosemion* species, this is the one that can most readily be recommended, because it is relatively problem free with regard to feeding, general care and breeding. It can be kept with fish of the same type. A shallow, well planted aquarium with a dark peat mulch on the bed is particularly suitable. Spawns on plants.

Name	**Red Lyretail** *(Aphyosemion bivittatum)*
Distribution range	Equatorial Africa, Togo, in jungle pools
Approx. size (fully grown)	$1^{1}/_{2}$ ins
Sexual differences	The males – which are very variable in colouring – have much brighter hues than the rather inconspicuous females.
Suitability/ difficulty for aquaria	Requires a lot of attention to its general care and feeding.
Recommended water conditions	Temperature: 68–78° F; pH: 6.0–6.5; GH: 1–6° dH
Diet	*TetraMin, TetraTips, Tetra FD Menu,* live *Artemia*
Some important pointers	A beautiful little fish that is peaceful and tolerant. Is easily kept together with other fish that like soft, acidic water and a peat mulch on the bed of the tank. This species likes to keep to the middle water zone. It spawns on plants.

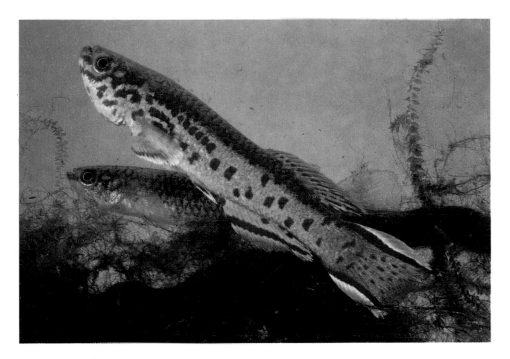

Name	**Steel Blue Aphyosemion** *(Aphyosemion gardneri)*
Distribution range	Africa, in the coastal regions of Nigeria
Approx. size (fully grown)	4 ins
Sexual differences	The male is much more intensely coloured and somewhat larger than the rather plain brown female.
Suitability/ difficulty for aquaria	Requires a lot of attention to its general care and feeding.
Recommended water conditions	Temperature: 68–78° F; pH: 6.5; GH: 5–8° dH
Diet	*TetraMin, TetraTips, Tetra FD Menu, TetraDelica Red Mosquito Larvae,* live *Artemia*
Some important pointers	A very beautiful species that is best kept in pairs because males are rather intolerant of one another. Smallish aquaria – and shallow ones at that – are adequate. A dark bed and background will enhance the effect of their magnificent colours. They lay their eggs in the peat mulch. These take around 22 days to develop at a temperature of 71° F and the young are not difficult to raise.

Name	**Striped Panchax** *(Aplocheilus lineatus)*
Distribution range	Peninsular India and Ceylon (Sri Lanka)
Approx. size (fully grown)	3 ins
Sexual differences	The colouring of the male is considerably more intense.
Suitability/ difficulty for aquaria	Requires a lot of attention to its general care and feeding.
Recommended water conditions	Temperature: 68–78° F; pH: 6.0–6.8; GH: up to 12° dH
Diet	*TetraMin,* live food
Some important pointers	A surface fish that can be very predatory in behaviour towards smaller species. Feels especially at home in a largish tank with a canopy of floating plants as it is rather light shy. Needs a high protein diet and its favourite food is small fish though it will also take small pieces of *TetraTips* from tweezers. Spawns in roots and floating plants.

Name	**Firemouth Epiplatys** (*Epiplatys dageti*)
Distribution range	Tropical West Africa from Liberia to Ghana
Approx. size (fully grown)	2 ins
Sexual differences	The throat is reddish in the male.
Suitability/ difficulty for aquaria	Not fussy in respect of either water or food.
Recommended water conditions	Temperature: 68–78° F; pH: 6.0–6.5; GH: up to 10° dH
Diet	*TetraMin, TetraDelica Red Mosquito Larvae*
Some important pointers	Very much a surface fish, peaceful and not at all timid. A very good sort for the planted community tank. Has no special requirements in terms of water quality and food which it prefers to take from the surface. It lays its eggs in the feathery fronds of plants.

Breeding egg-laying tooth carps is not particularly difficult provided you give them the right water conditions and feed them well. In the wild the majority of these fish have only a short life span. Because they occur in nature in quite small and shallow expanses of water that dry out during the drought season, the Killifish have evolved a reproductive technique to cope with these special circumstances. The adult fish spawn in pairs – though sometimes this may rise to several individuals together – shortly before the dry season sets in. The eggs are capable of withstanding the rigours of the drought enclosed in the moist bed of the pond (peat fibre / leaf litter) until the rains come again. The fry then hatch quickly and become sexually mature within eight months (approximately) – just before the onset of the dry season. With the lack of any dry season in the aquarium, Killifish may life to the ripe old age of two years.

Left column from above:
Nothobranchius melanospilus (an East African Killifish)
The male induces the female to spawn.
She starts to search for a suitable place; the male remains in close contact.
The male's attentions become more urgent.

Right column from above:
The male clasps the female with his dorsal fin.
Mating takes place.
Mating with two males.

Name	**Rachov's Nothobranchus** (*Nothobranchus rachovi*)
Distribution range	Mozambique (East Africa)
Approx. size (fully grown)	2 ins
Sexual differences	The female is a colourless greyish brown shade.
Suitability/ difficulty for aquaria	This can only be recommended for experienced hobbyists because it has special requirements in respect of water and food.
Recommended water conditions	Temperature: 71–78° F; pH: 6.5; GH: 4–6° dH
Diet	*TetraMin, Tetra FD Menu,* live *Artemia,* live food
Some important pointers	A very highly coloured seasonal fish. Once it has spawned the peat should be removed, passed through a fine sieve to dehydrate it, and then stored for about three months in a covered bowl at room temperature, keeping out most of the air. If rainwater is then poured over it at a temperature of about 71–75° F, the fry will hatch in succession over a period of less than a week.

Family Poeciliidae

Group 6: **Family Poeciliidae**
Livebearing Tooth Carps

All these species are restricted primarily to Central and South America. Fish belonging to this genus are readily recognised by the anal fin of the male which has evolved into a reproductive organ known as the 'gonopodium'. In some species the females display the so-called gravid/pregnancy mark on the rear part of her belly.

According to the different species, but also dependent upon the temperature, the period of gestation varies between 4 to 6 weeks. The female takes in the sperm in a sperm sac and it will remain viable for a fairly lengthy time in this. This means that the stored sperm can be used to fertilise eggs for a number of successive pregnancies, without any need for renewed copulation with a male. The young fish – $^1/_4$–$^1/_2$ ins long, depending on the species – leave their mother's body in the perfectly formed state. They will immediately start to take fine food and are easily raised on a diet of *Tetra Baby Fish Foods* or very finely sieved *TetraMin,* supplemented with *Artemia* nauplia.

Anyone wishing to go into breeding these fish in a serious way should keep the pregnant females separately in small (entirely glass) aquaria, furnished with dense clumps of plants. The latter will enable the young fish to flee from the cannibalistic attentions of their mother, a form of behaviour that is all too frequently seen. Once the birth process is complete, the mother can be removed and the fry raised separately. Aquarium shops offer so called breeding traps that can be set up inside the main aquarium.

The livebearers are undemanding subjects from every standpoint, many species being absolutely ideal for the beginner. However, there are still many experienced experts who have already managed to cope with the most difficult of the 'problem fish' who still go in for keeping and breeding these varieties. The fascination that these fish hold for breeders is, in fact, that some genera have a marked tendency to produce variable offspring.

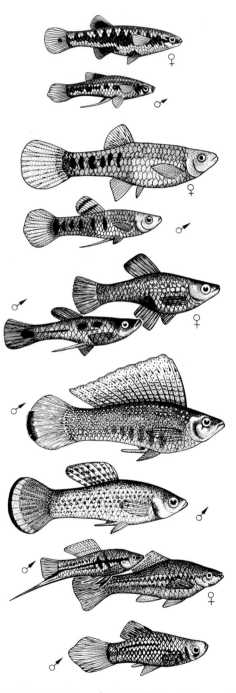

Typical body forms of the family Poeciliidae

Name	**Sailfin Molly** (*Poecilia latipinna*)
Distribution range	Mexico, Texas
Approx. size (fully grown)	4 ins
Sexual differences	The high dorsal fin of the male, and he also has a gonopodium.
Suitability/ difficulty for aquaria	Not fussy in respect of either water or food.
Recommended water conditions	Temperature: 71–82° F; pH: 7.0–8.2; GH: 15–30° dH
Diet	*Tetra Conditioning Food, TetraTips,* algae
Some important pointers	A decorative, peaceable sort. If it is to reach its full potential it requires a large aquarium with plants, bright lighting and plenty of algal growth. Also to be recommended is the addition of some sea salt to achieve slightly brackish conditions (perhaps 1–2 heaped teaspoons per two gallons) under which *Vallisneria* may also continue to thrive. Good as a companion for guppies and the smaller species of labyrinth fish. The very similar species, *Poecilia velifera,* is even more impressive but requires a still larger tank with lots of algae on which to feed if it is to develop fully. The photograph shows a pretty hybrid form of this species.

Name	**Black Bellied Limia** (*Poecilia melanogaster*)
Distribution range	Jamaica, Haiti
Approx. size (fully grown)	2 ins
Sexual differences	The female has a large bluey-black gravid mark.
Suitability/ difficulty for aquaria	Not fussy in respect of either water or food.
Recommended water conditions	Temperature: 68–78° F; pH: 7.5–8.5; GH: 20–30° dH
Diet	*Tetra Conditioning Food, TetraTips,* algae
Some important pointers	A species with interesting markings. Well suited to the community tank. Provide plenty of places of refuge because the males can be over attentive at times. An excellent fish for keeping algae under control, and will suffer if it does not have a good supply. So the tank should be well lit (direct sunlight for some of the day). In the early stages the young fish are fast growing but then need more than six months before they take on their final colouring.

Name	**Guppy** *(Poecilia reticulata)*
Distribution range	South America, north of the Amazon and the offshore islands of Trinidad and Barbados
Approx. size (fully grown)	$1^1/_2$ ins, hybrid forms reaching $2^1/_2$ ins
Sexual differences	The male is much smaller than the female. It is also much more brightly coloured and has a gonopodium.
Suitability/ difficulty for aquaria	Not fussy in respect of either water or food.
Recommended water conditions	Temperature: 71–82° F; pH: 7.0–8.5; GH: 20–30° dH
Diet	*TetraMin, Tetra FD Menu, TetraTips,* live *Artemia*
Some important pointers	One of the earliest aquarium fish. The wild form – scarcely found at all in the trade nowadays – is easily satisfied, a tough little sort and very fertile. The beautiful hybrid forms are more demanding and require careful monitoring of their water and feeding. See illustrations overleaf.

The photographs show hybrid forms of guppies

Top: Fantail
Middle: Triangle
Bottom: Vienna Emerald

The left hand column shows various standard guppy hybrid forms (from above):

Round tail, Needle tail, Pointed tail, Spade tail, Lyre tail, Top sword, Bottom sword, Double sword, Flag sword, Veil tail, Fantail, Triangle tail

Name	**Black Molly** *(Poecilia sphenops)*
Distribution range	Mexico to Venezuela (wild form)
Approx. size (fully grown)	$2^1/_2$ ins
Sexual differences	The male is smaller and has the gonopodium.
Suitability/ difficulty for aquaria	Not fussy in respect of either water or food.
Recommended water conditions	Temperature: 71–82° F; pH: 7.5–8.2; GH: 18–30° dH
Diet	*TetraMin, Tetra Conditioning Food, TetraTips*
Some important pointers	The very popular Black Molly is a hybrid of a natural form which has a bluish shimmering colour overlaid with a silver green sheen. Checkered forms also exist. Is easy to breed in the community tank if the young fish can find plenty of hideouts in which to take refuge in the early stages of their life and they have a constant supply of food. These fish like lots of food and warmth. A corner filled with floating plants like aquatic fern will make the task of raising the young fry easier.

Name	**Lyre Tail Black Molly** *(Poecilia sphenops)*
Distribution range	Hybrid form
Approx. size (fully grown)	$2^1/_2$ ins
Sexual differences	The male is smaller and has a gonopodium.
Suitability/ difficulty for aquaria	Not fussy in respect of either water or food.
Recommended water conditions	Temperature: 75–82° F; pH: 7.0–8.5; GH: 15–30° dH
Diet	*TetraMin, Tetra Conditioning Food, TetraTips*
Some important pointers	This hybrid form is rather more of a heat lover than the previous variety and requires careful feeding. Feed frequently when still growing. Hard water or slightly brackish water will help promote good development. Adult fish not fussy. One or two teaspoons of marine salt per two gallons is normally adequate.

Name	**Green Swordtail** (*Xiphophorus helleri*)
Distribution range	Mexico, Guatemala
Approx. size (fully grown)	$3^1/_2$ ins
Sexual differences	The male carries a sword-like extension to the tail fin and has the gonopodium.
Suitability/ difficulty for aquaria	Not fussy in respect of either water or food.
Recommended water conditions	Temperature: 68–78° F; pH: 7.0–8.3; GH: 12–30° dH
Diet	*TetraTips, TetraMin, Tetra Conditioning Food*
Some important pointers	The original wild form. A very beautiful, gracious and undemanding aquarium fish, that is suitable for the community tank and for the beginner. The males are apt to put on a very skillful swimming display around the female during which they may even swim backwards. A peaceful sort. These fish will only grow to their full splendour and size if they are given careful filtration, frequent additions of fresh water and careful feeding. The fry need regular live *Artemia* to do well.

Name	**Red Swordtail** (*Xiphophorus helleri*)
Distribution range	Hybrid form
Approx. size (fully grown)	$3^1/_2$ ins
Sexual differences	The male carries a sword-like extension to the tail fin and has the gonopodium.
Suitability/ difficulty for aquaria	Not fussy in respect of either water or food.
Recommended water conditions	Temperature: 71–78° F; pH: 7.0–8.3; GH: 12–30° dH
Diet	*TetraTips, TetraMin, Tetra Conditioning Food*
Some important pointers	One of the most popular of the numerous hybrid forms of swordtails. In all sexually mature females of this species and its hybrid forms there is a dark looking gravid mark on the rear part of the body, which is very visible. A decorative fish for the community tank.

Name	**Simpson's Swordtail** *(Xiphophorus helleri)*
Distribution range	Hybrid form
Approx. size (fully grown)	$3^1/_2$ ins
Approx. size (fully grown)	See Swordtail
Suitability/ difficulty for aquaria	Not fussy in respect of either water or food.
Recommended water conditions	Temperature: 71–78° F; pH: 7.0–8.3; GH: 12–30° dH
Diet	*TetraMin, Tetra Conditioning Food, TetraTips*
Some important pointers	In general, as for the previously described forms. This *Xiphophorus,* lends itself especially to genetic experiments and observations. All the forms are capable of being cross-bred with the others, and bear fertile offspring. Generally speaking, the hybrid forms do not have the robustness of the wild form and for this reason the fry should be raised separately.

Name	**Red or Coral Platy** (*Xiphophorus maculatus*)
Distribution range	Mexico, Guatemala
Approx. size (fully grown)	2 ins
Sexual differences	The male has a gonopodium.
Suitability/ difficulty for aquaria	Not fussy in respect of either water or food.
Recommended water conditions	Temperature: 71–78° F; pH: 7.0–8.2; GH: 10–25° dH
Diet	*TetraMin, Tetra Conditioning Food, TetraTips*
Some important pointers	The self coloured Platies that are kept in the aquarium are for the most part hybrid forms. They are pretty, undemanding fish that are suitable for keeping together with the widest possible range of other fish. An especially popular sort is the Red or Coral Platy which makes a splendid contrast to the green of plants and the Black Molly.

Name	**Variable or Sunset Platy** *(Xiphophorus variatus)*
Distribution range	Mexico
Approx. size (fully grown)	$2^{1}/_{2}$ ins
Sexual differences	The male has a gonopodium.
Suitability/ difficulty for aquaria	Not fussy in respect of either water or food.
Recommended water conditions	Temperature: 65–75° F; pH: 7.0–8.3; GH: 15– 30° dH
Diet	*TetraMin, Tetra Conditioning Food, TetraTips*
Some important pointers	Shown here is the original form which is only occasionally available through the trade. The main reason for this is that the young fish are initially rather dull, grey looking items and remain so for the first eight to twelve months of their lives, until they are almost fully grown. These grey juveniles are, almost understandably, poor sellers because the potential purchaser has no idea of how the 'ugly duckling' will turn out.

Name	**Black Platy** (*Xiphophorus variatus*)
Distribution range	Hybrid form
Approx. size (fully grown)	$2^{1}/_{2}$ ins
Sexual differences	The male has a gonopodium.
Suitability/ difficulty for aquaria	Not fussy in respect of either water or food.
Recommended water conditions	Temperature: 65–75° F; pH: 7.0–8.3; GH: 15–30° dH
Diet	*TetraMin, Tetra Conditioning Food, TetraTips*
Some important pointers	General details are similar to those for the Variable Platy. All forms of this species will dwindle away if they do not get a steady supply of plant food and if kept too warm. Fluctuations dropping to 60° F and below (53° F occasionally) are tolerated. As such, this species diverges from the other *Xiphophorus* species and should not be kept at random in company with other warmth loving fish species.

Name	**Mosquito Fish, Dwarf Livebearer** *(Heterandria formosa)*
Distribution range	South Carolina to Florida (North America)
Approx. size (fully grown)	$^3/_4$ ins
Sexual differences	The male is smaller with a gonopodium.
Suitability/ difficulty for aquaria	Not difficult but do follow the hints on feeding.
Recommended water conditions	Temperature: 68–78° F; pH: 6.8–7.5; GH: 5–20° dH
Diet	*TetraMin, Tetra FD Menu,* live *Artemia*
Some important pointers	The smallest tropical fish and one of the smallest of all vertebrates. Very small aquaria with parts planted very densely are adequate. Harmless and undemanding, it is only suitable for the community tank under certain conditions because it will soon be overwhelmed and lost because of its tiny size. Two or three young are born every day over an eight day period – a process that is repeated every four to five weeks.

Suborder Siluroidei

Group 7: **Suborder Siluroidei**
Catfish

Out of the many families and genera of catfish there are relatively few species that have found a lasting place in the amateur's aquarium. In those cases where they have become accepted it is often because of their bizarre, often grotesque appearance – they can often be simply described as 'funny' – or because of their supposed usefullness as scavengers for various bits of tank debris.

There are, however, many predatory species of catfish and these have understandably found it difficult to win over the hearts of the fish hobbyist.

Catfish are scaleless, occasionally quite naked, and usually covered with bony plates. Most of them are decidedly bottom fish and spend their time – usually at night – scouring the tank bed for titbits of food and chewing over the accumulated debris. The armoured catfish in particular need a soft, fine sanded bed, at least in that part of the aquarium where they are fed. All species have barbels or whiskers that act as sensory and olfactory organs. If the bed of the tank were to be hard gravel, they would abrade these sense organs to the point where they turn into cripples. So in accordance with the overall purpose of this volume, only those species are being presented that are suited to the community tank, disregarding those that can be more correctly regarded as interesting subjects for study in the hands of specialists.

The species shown here belong to the following families:

Arriidae
Asprenidae   Frying pan catfish
Callinchthyidae   Armoured Catfish   (C)
Loricariidae   (Lo)
Mochokidae   (M)
Pimelodidae
Schilbeidae   (S)

An alternative classification elevates the Catfish as a group to the order Siluriformes.

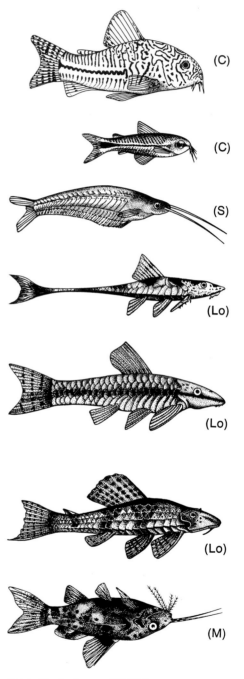

Typical body shapes of Catfish

Name	**Arius or Saltwater Catfish** *(Arius seemani)*
Distribution range	From California through Mexico to Colombia, in rivers flowing into the Pacific
Approx. size (fully grown)	12 ins
Sexual differences	Not discernable in young specimens. Older females of spawning age are noticeably fuller in the belly than the males.
Suitability/ difficulty for aquaria	Requires a lot of attention to general care and feeding.
Recommended water conditions	Temperature: 71–78° F; pH: 7.0–8.0; GH: up to 30° dH
Diet	Flaked food from the water surface; *TetraTips* and *TabiMin* and any kind of live food.
Some important pointers	Those species of fish that bear a resemblance to sharks have always tempted fishkeepers into buying them. As a juvenile this species is very easy to please, but later requires a great deal of attention to its general care: for instance, it then needs about half to two-thirds strength seawater (with a specific gravity around 1.012–1.016). This makes them rather unsuitable for the normal community tank once they have reached a length of 6 ins or so. There are few details of any breeding successes. It is probable that they spawn in brackish water.

Name	**Frying-Pan or Banjo Catfish** (*Bunocephalus knerii*)
Distribution range	Inundated areas of the Amazon floodplain in the rain forest (South America)
Approx. size (fully grown)	$3^{1}/_{2}$ ins
Sexual differences	Not discernable
Suitability/ difficulty for aquaria	Not difficult but it does have some specific require-ments in respect of the water conditions and tank decoration.
Recommended water conditions	Temperature: 68–78° F; pH: 5.8–7.0; GH: 3–8° dH
Diet	*TabiMin, TetraTips FD, TetraDelica Red Mosquito Larvae,* deep frozen food
Some important pointers	These fish are sensitive to light and require well planted aquaria with plenty of hideouts. A sandy corner should be set up for them to bury themselves in. It is also an advantage if they have a cover of floating plants to reduce light levels. Otherwise the species is accom-modating and peaceable and can be kept together with all other more placid species of fish.

Name	**Bronze Catfish** (*Corydoras aeneus*)
Distribution range	Venezuela, Trinidad to La Plata
Approx. size (fully grown)	$2^1/_2$ ins
Sexual differences	Males are larger and have a more pointed dorsal fin.
Suitability/ difficulty for aquaria	Not fussy in respect of either water or food.
Recommended water conditions	Temperature: 71–82° F; pH: 6.0–8.0; GH: 2–25° dH
Diet	*TetraMin, Tetra Conditioning Food, TetraTips, Tabi-Min*
Some important pointers	A peaceful, funny little bottom fish that likes to keep company with other members of its own species. Like other species of *Corydoras*, it can fetch air from the water surface for intestinal breathing, and prefers a sandy or humus covered bed that it can dig in, stirring up the material to quite an extent. Just a couple of specimens of almost all of these *Corydoras* species are suited to the community tank (although a species shoal is better) and, as they are omnivorous, will readily consume any leftovers. Quite possible to breed them.

Name	**Arched Corydoras** *(Corydoras arcuatus)*
Distribution range	The Amazone region
Approx. size (fully grown)	$2^1/_2$ ins
Sexual differences	Males are larger and have a more pointed dorsal fin.
Suitability/ difficulty for aquaria	Not fussy in respect of either water or food.
Recommended water conditions	Temperature: 71–82° F; pH: 6.0–8.0; GH: 2–25° dH
Diet	*TetraMin, Tetra Conditioning Food, TetraTips, Tabi-Min*
Some important pointers	A peaceful bottom fish that likes the company of other members of its species. These small armoured catfish can be kept in a mixed species shoal. It is possible to breed these and they stick their eggs to stones like other *Corydoras* species. Raising the young *Corydoras* gives a great deal of pleasure though the young fish require fine live food as their diet.

Name	**Dwarf Corydoras** *(Corydoras hastatus)*
Distribution range	The Amazon region
Approx. size (fully grown)	1¹/₄ ins
Sexual differences	Very difficult to distinguish
Suitability/ difficulty for aquaria	Not difficult but do follow the hints on feeding.
Recommended water conditions	Temperature: 75–82° F; pH: 6.0–7.8; GH: 2–25° dH
Diet	*TetraMin, TetraTips, Tetra FD Menu,* live *Artemia*
Some important pointers	A small, charming and pretty armoured catfish that is a lively swimmer, moving around the free water zone in a shoal. This fish is a must for every small community tank. It likes old water that does not contain too much nitrate, and so fresh water should be added occasionally. Breeding possible. Often confused with *C. pygmaeus,* the somewhat rarer Pigmy Corydoras.

Name	**Black-spotted Corydoras** (*Corydoras melanistius*)
Distribution range	British Guyana, probably also the Amazon region, tributaries of the Rio Madeira
Approx. size (fully grown)	$2^1/_2$ ins
Sexual differences	Unknown
Suitability/ difficulty for aquaria	Not fussy in respect of either water or food.
Recommended water conditions	Temperature: 71–82° F; pH: 6.0–8.0; GH: 2–25° dH
Diet	*TetraMin, TabiMin, TetraTips*
Some important pointers	As a bottom dwelling fish, this is suitable for the community tank. It needs fine, dark sand as a bed covering. The *Corydoras* species are found predominantly in the shallower, quieter bank zones of small streams and medium sized rivers. They always live a communal lifestyle, in little shoals. Very often two or more species occur together though the individual species will remain together within a shoal.

Name	**Peppered Corydoras** *(Corydoras paleatus)*
Distribution range	Southern Brazil, La Plata
Approx. size (fully grown)	$2^1/_2$ ins
Sexual differences	The male has a high, notched dorsal fin.
Suitability/ difficulty for aquaria	Not fussy in respect of either water or food.
Recommended water conditions	Temperature: 68–78° F; pH: 6.0–8.0; GH: 2–25° dH
Diet	*TetraMin, TabiMin, TetraTips*
Some important pointers	The most durable and hardy of the armoured catfish, otherwise as for the previously described species. You should ensure that *Corydoras* species are not kept on a hard edged gravel bed or they will easily damage their mouth barbels. Breeding is possible.

Name	**Pigmy Corydoras** (*Corydoras pygmaeus*)
Distribution range	Amazon region
Approx. size (fully grown)	1 ins
Sexual differences	Unknown
Suitability/ difficulty for aquaria	Requires a lot of attention to its general care and feeding.
Recommended water conditions	Temperature: 75–82° F; pH: 6.0–8.0; GH: 2–25° dH
Diet	*TetraMin, Tetra FD Menu, TetraTips,* live *Artemia*
Some important pointers	This rather rare, dwarf species of *Corydoras* is similar in behaviour to *C. hastatus*. Unlike other *Corydoras*, these two species like to swim in the middle water zones at times. It is not advisable to keep these little fellows with other larger fish, because they are often regarded as prey and pursued the length and breadth of the aquarium.

Name	**Leopard Corydoras** *(Corydoras trilineatus)*
Distribution range	The smaller tributaries of the middle Amazon
Approx. size (fully grown)	$2^1/_2$ ins
Sexual differences	Difficult to distinguish.
Suitability/ difficulty for aquaria	Not fussy in respect of either water or food.
Recommended water conditions	Temperature: 71–82° F; pH: 6.0–8.0; GH: 2–25° dH
Diet	*TetraMin, Tetra Conditioning Food, TetraTips, Tabi-Min*
Some important pointers	Another lively bottom fish that likes to live in a shoal. Otherwise as for the previous species. Breeding successes with this have been few and far between. The very similar species, *C. julii,* from the lower reaches of the Amazon is only infrequently encountered through dealers.

Name	**Bristle-nosed Catfish** *(Ancistrus dolichopterus)*
Distribution range	Clear streams and tributaries of the Amazon (South America)
Approx. size (fully grown)	$5^1/_2$ ins
Sexual differences	The males are markedly larger than the females and have pronounced growths on their heads.
Suitability/ difficulty for aquaria	Not fussy in respect of either water or food.
Recommended water conditions	Temperature: 71–80° F; pH: 6.5–7.5; GH: 5–20° dH
Diet	*TetraTips, TetraMin*, peas and algae. Feed in the evening.
Some important pointers	These fish are easily cared for and catered for. However, they do require well filtered water and a number of caves/crevices to hide in under bogwood and rocks. They are easy to breed. Their orange coloured eggs are laid in a hollow or cavity where the male will watch over them. The fry are then raised on algae, squashed peas, *TetraTips* and powdered fry foods.

Name	**Sucker-mouth Catfish, Plecostomus** *(Hypostomus punctatus)*
Distribution range	Brazil
Approx. size (fully grown)	Up to 8 ins
Sexual differences	Unknown
Suitability/ difficulty for aquaria	Not fussy in respect of either water or food.
Recommended water conditions	Temperature: 68–78° F; pH: 5.8–7.5; GH: up to 25° dH
Diet	*TetraTips*
Some important pointers	A peaceful, curious and interesting bottom fish that is usually rather timid, feeding only at night. Likes dark corners amongst plants and roots where it can hide away. Otherwise it lies resting on rocks, plant leaves or the tank bottom. Is not an over zealous digger when searching for food. Very little is known about its repro-duction.

Name	**Sucker Catfish** (*Otocinclus vittatus*)
Distribution range	Brazil
Approx. size (fully grown)	$1^1/_2$ ins
Sexual differences	The female is rounder than the male.
Suitability/ difficulty for aquaria	Not fussy in respect of either water or food.
Recommended water conditions	Temperature: 68–78° F; pH: 5.5–7.2; GH: up to 15° dH
Diet	*TetraMin, Tetra Conditioning Food, TetraTips*
Some important pointers	A peaceful fish that usually spends its time sliding over broad leaved plants or the panes of the aquarium, devouring the layer of algae there. Likes plenty of hideouts in dense clumps of vegetation. A suitable subject for the community tank if its companions are reasonably placid.

Name	**Whiptail Catfish** *(Rineloricaria microlepidogaster)*
Distribution range	Paraguay, La Plata
Approx. size (fully grown)	$4^1/_2$ ins
Sexual differences	The males have a set of bristles at the sides of their heads.
Suitability/ difficulty for aquaria	Not difficult
Recommended water conditions	Temperature: 71–82° F; pH: 5.8–6.8; GH: up to 15° dH
Diet	*TetraMin, TetraTips*
Some important pointers	A peaceable, undemanding bottom fish with a very interesting body shape. Loves a calm lifestyle, scarcely moving at all during the day but at night scouring the entire aquarium for scraps of food. It disturbs only the very uppermost surface of the tank bed. It likes dark corners amongst plants (though not *too* densely planted) and cavities amongst roots. Suitable for a community tank that contains just a low stock of fish. Spawns in narrow crevices and looks after its brood.

Fish catchers in a Brazilian catfish habitat.

Name	**Upside down Catfish** *(Synodontis nigriventris)*
Distribution range	Africa, the Congo
Approx. size (fully grown)	3¹/₂ ins
Sexual differences	The male is slimmer than the rather plump female.
Suitability/ difficulty for aquaria	Requires a lot of attention to its general care and feeding.
Recommended water conditions	Temperature: 71–82° F; pH: 6.5–7.5; GH: up to 20° dH
Diet	*TetraMin, TetraTips*
Some important pointers	A peaceful shoaling fish that often swims on its back. It leads a very retiring lifestyle and is only active at night. It is also possible to keep just a single specimen. In a community tank it should only be kept with larger fish. Prefers caves, dark places under roots and rocks or large leaved plants. This fish is undemanding, hardy and a very interesting subject to observe. Little is known about its reproduction though it probably lays its eggs in cavities, like for instance, flowerpots. Few breeding successes have been heard of.

Name	**Polka-dot Catfish** *(Pimelodus pictus)*
Distribution range	Colombia (South America)
Approx. size (fully grown)	$4^1/_2$ ins
Sexual differences	Not visible
Suitability/ difficulty for aquaria	Not difficult, but do follow the hints on feeding.
Recommended water conditions	Temperature: 71–76° F; pH: 5.8–7.5; GH: 6–15° dH
Diet	*TabiMin, TetraTips, Tetra FD Menu, TetraMin.* Only feed in the twilight hours.
Some important pointers	This is a species that is most active at night, and thus prefers an aquarium with subdued light and a cover of floating plants. It also needs peat extracts added to its water. Plenty of cavities under rocks, wood and bog-wood roots are also desirable. These fish are peaceable but an occasion may nolest smaller species of fish. However, they may be tempted to regard small fry as morsels of live food. Powerful filtration with a good current of water is advisable.

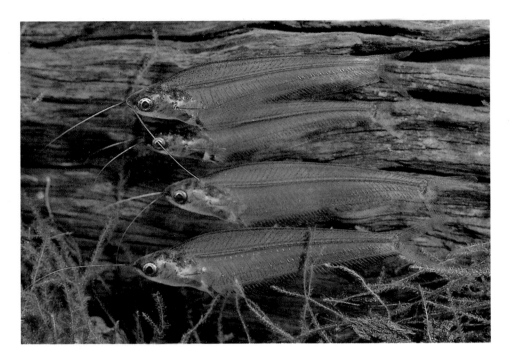

Name	**Glass Catfish** *(Kryptopterus bicirrhis)*
Distribution range	Indonesia, Borneo, Sumatra, Thailand
Approx. size (fully grown)	4 ins
Sexual differences	Unknown
Suitability/ difficulty for aquaria	Requires a lot of attention to its general care and feeding.
Recommended water conditions	Temperature: 71–82° F; pH: 6.0–7.5; GH: 5–15° dH
Diet	*TetraMin, Tetra FD Menu,* live food.
Some important pointers	A delicate, almost transparent shoaling fish with a strange glass-like quality. Always keep a number of them together. Likes a roomy, not too light aquarium with vegetation that is not too dense. It is only advisable to keep these with other fish that are equally delicate. Little information available about their breeding, although aquarium breeding has been recorded.

Fish From Other Families

Group 8: **Fish from other families**

Throughout the world there are probably around 350 million tropical fish in the hands of amateur fish hobbyists at any given time. Over half of these are accounted for by just 25 species and over three quarters by some 50 species and hybrids.

Many owners of aquaria do not even know the names and families of their fish at all, which is rather a regrettable situation though not all that surprising and in some senses quite understandable. The idea and purpose underlying this volume is to try to remedy this to some extent by arousing interest through a stimulating presentation both in words and pictures, and by the easily understandable classification method used.

As already mentioned there are a few species that do not fit into the seven main groups that have been presented up to now.

These species are classified into the following families:

Atherinidae	Rainbow fish, Silverfish	(At)
Centropomidae	Glassfish	(Cp)
Exocoetidae	Flying Fish and related species	(Ex)
Gobiidae	Gobies	(Go)
Mastacembelidae	Spiney Eels	(Ma)
Melanotaeniidae	Rainbow Fish	(Me)
Mormyridae	Elephant Fish	(Mo)
Pantodontidae	Butterfly Fish	(Mm)
Scatophagidae	Argus Fish	(Pa)
Tetraodontidae	Pufferfish or Globe Fish	(Sc)

As will be seen below, some of these fish prefer slightly brackish water. This was discussed earlier, and in relation to the *Arius* Catfish and some livebearers (Family Poeciliidae). Naturally, many community fish (and plants) do not enjoy even slightly salty water, and even any change in the salinity (or 'saltiness') must be done gradually. For information, note that full strength seawater is equivalent *(very approximately)* to 15 heaped teaspoons of marine salt per gallon, and should result in a specific gravity of around 1.024 (at 75° F).

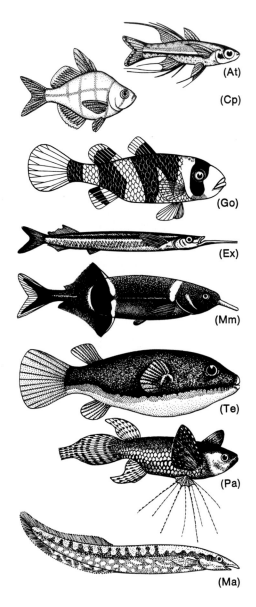

Some body forms of fish in group 8

Name	**Madagascan Rainbowfish** *(Bedotia geayi)*
Distribution range	Madagascar
Approx. size (fully grown)	3¹/₂ ins
Sexual differences	The male has a dark red 'hem' to its fins.
Suitability/ difficulty for aquaria	Not fussy in respect of either water or food.
Recommended water conditions	Temperature: 71–78° F; pH: 7–8; GH: 10–20° dH
Diet	*TetraMin, TetraDelica Red Mosquito Larvae*
Some important pointers	A very lively, singular type of shoaling fish, well suited to the community tank. Loves lots of free swimming space, with background and edge planting. Unfortunately it grows to quite a large size. Likes hard water and frequent additions of fresh water. A free spawner. Easy to breed and raise.

Name	**Celebes Rainbowfish** *(Telmatherina ladigesi)*
Distribution range	Celebes
Approx. size (fully grown)	$2^1/_2$ ins
Sexual differences	The first ray of the male's dorsal and anal fin is elongated.
Suitability/ difficulty for aquaria	Only to be recommended for experienced fishkeepers because it has special requirements in respect ot its feeding and water quality.
Recommended water conditions	Temperature: 71–78° F; pH: 7.2–8.0; GH: 12–30° dH
Diet	*TetraMin, Tetra FD Menu,* live *Artemia*
Some important pointers	A lively, cheerful shoaling fish that lives in the middle water zone and loves plenty of free swimming room. Sensitive to soft, old water (frequent additions of fresh water needed). A bit of an 'expert's' fish! The harder the water the better for this one. Where the hardness is under 20° dH, sea salt should be added ($^1/_2$ to 1 heaped teaspoon of marine salt per 2 gallons). Consequently its suitability for a community tank is rather limited. It is also susceptible to parasite attack.

Name	**Indian Glassfish** *(Chanda ranga)*
Distribution range	Eastern India, Burma, Thailand
Approx. size (fully grown)	$1^1/_2$ ins
Sexual differences	The easily visible swim bladder is round at the rear in the female and pointed in the male.
Suitability/ difficulty for aquaria	Requires a lot of attention to its general care and feeding.
Recommended water conditions	Temperature: 64–77° F; pH: 7.0–8.0
Diet	*TetraMin, Tetra FD Menu,* mainly live food
Some important pointers	A peaceful, very dainty looking fish which is, however, rather shy, although it is a shoaling fish. It should, therefore, only be kept together with smaller more placid species. It prefers dense clumps of plants but with some free swimming room and a dark tank bed. Lives in the middle water zone. Attaches its eggs at points in between plants. It will breed but raising the young is difficult. Best in brackish water so salt should be added at 1–2 heaped teaspoons of marine salt per two gallons.

Name	**Halfbeak** *(Dermogenys pusillus)*
Distribution range	Thailand, Malaya, Great Sunda Islands
Approx. size (fully grown)	3 ins
Sexual differences	The male's anal fin has evolved to some extent into a reproductive organ.
Suitability/ difficulty for aquaria	Requires a lot of attention to its general care and feeding.
Recommended water conditions	Temperature: 75–82° F; pH: around 7.0; GH: up to 10° dH
Diet	*TetraMin, Tetra FD Menu,* live food (flying insects).
Some important pointers	A surface dwelling fish that hunts after insects mainly but also little young fish. Apart from this it is suitable for the community tank. It is best if a number of them are kept together. Prefers a light cover of floating plants. A dashing swimmer that does, however, like to stand still occasionally. The male is pugnacious and is used in competitive fights in its native country. A livebearer. Additions of sea salt are necessary for breeding as it occurs in brackish water too (2–3 heaped teaspoons of marine salt per 2 gallons). Plants will not tolerate this degree of salinity very well.

Name	**Belted Spiny Eel** *(Mastacembelus circumcinctus)*
Distribution range	South East Asia
Approx. size (fully grown)	10 ins
Sexual differences	The female is more powerfully built.
Suitability/ difficulty for aquaria	Requires a lot of attention to its general care and feeding.
Recommended water conditions	Temperature: 73–82° F; pH: around 7.0; GH: up to 15° dH
Diet	Live food, *TetraMin, TetraTips*
Some important pointers	Sometimes these spiny eels become very confiding in captivity. If they do not overcome their natural timidity, they lead a secretive life around the bed of the tank, only venturing out to feed when evening approaches. In the community tank it should only be kept with larger fish. It should be given fine sand to bury itself in and a flowerpot as a refuge. Also advisable are additions of sea salt at $^1/_2$ heaped teaspoon per 2 gallons of water together with regular additions of new water with *AquaSafe*.

Name	**Boesemann's Rainbow Fish** *(Melanotaenia boesemani)*
Distribution range	New Guinea (Irian-Jaya i.e. the western part of the island).
Approx. size (fully grown)	4 ins
Sexual differences	The male is higher backed and is significantly more deeply coloured.
Suitability/ difficulty for aquaria	Not difficult but do follow the hints on feeding.
Recommended water conditions	Temperature: 80–86° F; pH: 7.5–9.0; GH: 7–18° dH
Diet	*TetraMin, TetraRuby, TetraDelica Red Mosquito Larvae*
Some important pointers	Fortunately, this magnificent species is raised in commercial quantities in captivity, for in the wild it is rather uncommon. It takes a full year for it to develop its full colouring as shown in the photo. It is a shoaling fish that should always be kept in numbers around the 3–7 mark, and in the company of other peaceful fish. They are darting little fish and good jumpers so the aquarium should always be kept well covered. The species (a continuous spawner) is easy to breed if provided with sufficient food for the growing youngsters (infusorians). Moderate levels of plants of a fine fronded type required.

Name	**Dwarf or Black-lined Rainbowfish** *(Melanotaenia macculochii)*
Distribution range	North Australia
Approx. size (fully grown)	3 ins
Sexual differences	The male is more colourful and higher backed than the female.
Suitability/ difficulty for aquaria	Not fussy in respect of either water or food.
Recommended water conditions	Temperature: 64–78° F; pH: 7.5–8; GH: 10–30° dH
Diet	*TetraMin, TetraRuby*
Some important pointers	A very lively, boldly marked, peaceful shoaling fish. It is easily catered for and quite hardy. Feasible subject for keeping in the community tank. Likes free swimming room in the middle and upper water zones. The plants should be set out either at the rear or the sides of the aquarium, according to taste. Likes frequent additions of fresh water, and prefers hard water. A free spawner. It is possible to breed these quite easily and in a largish aquarium with only a low level of fish in it, success is highly likely. Several other species of *Melanotaenia* are now available to hobbyists.

Name	**Fingerfish or Moon Fish** (*Monodactylus argenteus*)
Distribution range	The coasts of South East Asia, East Africa, the Red Sea
Approx. size (fully grown)	6 ins or even larger
Sexual differences	Not known
Suitability/ difficulty for aquaria	Only to be recommended for experienced fishkeepers because they have special requirements in respect of water conditions and feeding. Otherwise quite hardy.
Recommended water conditions	Temperature: 75–82° F; pH: 7.5–8.5; GH: 20–40° dH
Diet	*TetraMin, Tetra Conditioning Food, Tetra FD Menu,* live food
Some important pointers	These are quick, dashing, shoaling fish that need a lot of free swimming room and which should only be kept in groups. Young fish (up to $1^{1}/_{2}$ ins long) can be kept in fresh water with just slight additions of sea salt (1 heaped teaspoon per 2 gallons). Larger specimens require higher concentrations of salt, and the adult fish ought to have full strength seawater. Do not plant the aquarium. Very nitrite sensitive and so frequent partial water changes should be carried out with the appropriate additions of marine salt and *AquaSafe*.

Name	**Elephant-nose** (*Gnathonemus petersii*)
Distribution range	Africa from the Congo to the Niger
Approx. size (fully grown)	10 ins
Sexual differences	Unknown
Suitability/ difficulty for aquaria	Requires a lot of attention to its general care and feeding.
Recommended water conditions	Temperature: 71–82° F; pH: 6.5–7.5; GH: 6–18° dH
Diet	*TetraMin,* live food, frozen food
Some important pointers	Peaceable towards members of other species but weaker specimens of the same species are picked on. Territorial in the aquarium. A nocturnal fish that does become active at daytime as it becomes accustomed to aquarium life. Needs dense planting with a good supply of hideouts. Digs for its food and in doing so churns up the tank bed so that a fine sandy bed is essential. Suitable for the community tank. Likes old water with occasional additions of fresh water. No aquarium breeding successes have been recorded to date. Other Elephant-nose species are available from time to time.

Name	**Butterfly Fish** (*Pantodon buchholzi*)
Distribution range	West Africa from the Niger to the Congo
Approx. size (fully grown)	up to 6 ins
Sexual differences	The centre of the anal and caudal fins are extended in the male.
Suitability/ difficulty for aquaria	Requires a lot of attention to its general care and feeding.
Recommended water conditions	Temperature: 73–86° F; pH: around 6.5; GH: up to 15° dH
Diet	*TetraMin,* live food (meal worms and insects).
Some important pointers	A durable sort of surface fish with an unusual appearance. A *real* jumper so the aquarium should be covered with a well fitting lid. It is possible to keep this in a community tank but not with smaller fish. It likes to hide away under floating plants. Prefers soft water with peat filtration. Difficult to breed and raise.

Name	**Argus Fish or Scat** *(Scatophagus argus)*
Distribution range	Indo-Pacific (in the brackish water areas)
Approx. size (fully grown)	6 ins or even larger
Sexual differences	Unknown
Suitability/ difficulty for aquaria	Only recommended for experienced fishkeepers as it has special requirements in terms of water conditions and feeding. Otherwise quite hardy.
Recommended water conditions	Temperature: 75–82° F; pH: 7.5–8.5; GH: 0–20° dH please check hardness duoted
Diet	*TetraMin, Tetra Conditioning Food, Tetra FD Menu,* plants
Some important pointers	A shoaling fish of variable colouring that can at times be rather quarrelsome towards weaker members of the same species if the aquarium is too small. The Argus Fish is best kept in brackish water equivalent to one third seawater but it is also tolerant of full strength seawater. These fish cannot be recommended for fresh water tanks, and especially not for planted aquaria. The process of acclimating it from fresh to seawater or vice versa should be done gradually, over a period of say, a week. Very nitrite sensitive. No details of any breeding success in captivity are known.

Name	**Puffer Fish** (*Tetraodon lorteti*)
Distribution range	Thailand
Approx. size (fully grown)	3 ins
Sexual differences	When displaying the male raises a 'comb' on its back; his colouring also shows much more contrast and is brighter.
Suitability/ difficulty for aquaria	Requires a lot of attention to its general care and feeding.
Recommended water conditions	Temperature: 71–82° F; pH: 6–7.2; GH: 5–10° dH
Diet	*TetraMin, TetraTips*, live food (snails)
Some important pointers	A fresh water Puffer Fish. Up to a point it is suitable for the community tank, though not together with small fish. Good for clearing out any snail infestation. Prefers ramshorn and pond snails but not very hard shelled snails. This fish is also known as *Carinotetraodon somphongsi*.

Name	**Puffer Fish** *(Tetraodon steindachneri)*
Distribution range	Sumatra, Thailand
Approx. size (fully grown)	$3^1/_2$ ins
Sexual differences	Unknown
Suitability/ difficulty for aquaria	Requires a lot of attention to its general care and feeding.
Recommended water conditions	Temperature: 71–82° F; pH: 7.2–8.5; GH: 10–25° dH
Diet	Live food, frozen food, *TetraTips*, snails
Some important pointers	Like almost all the brackish water inhabiting Puffer Fish, this species also requires occasional additions of marine salt (at around $^1/_2$ heaped teaspoon per 2 gallons of water). They should be kept singly as they are inclined to bite one another. Their favourite food is snails, sucking the soft parts out of the shells. Will often bite holes in the leaves of aquatic plants trying to get at a snail on the other side. Not a fish for the novice.

Name	**Golden Banded Goby or Bumblebee Fish** *(Brachygobius xanthozona)*
Distribution range	Borneo, Indonesia
Approx. size (fully grown)	2 ins
Sexual differences	The female is usually rather fat.
Suitability/ difficulty for aquaria	Requires a lot of attention to its general care and feeding.
Recommended water conditions	Temperature: 71–82° F; pH: 7.5–8.5; GH: 20–30° dH
Diet	*TetraMin,* live food, live *Artemia*
Some important pointers	A placid, peaceful fish though it cannot be recommended for the community tank. It needs hard water or additions of marine salt at 1–3 heaped teaspoons per 2 gallons. Best in a species aquarium with hideouts under rocks and roots. Attaches its eggs in cavities. The male is very active in caring for the brood.

Index: English scientific names of fish

Index: English common names of fish

Picture Credits

All Photos by B. Kahl, exept
Dr. C. Andrews	6, 11, 13, 17, 29, 30, 36, 43, 45, 46, 47, 49, 51, 56, 62, 63
H. A. Baensch	113
O. Böhm	206
Dr. W. Försch	234
H. Linke	55, 120, 128, 133, 135
M. Meyer	122
H. J. Mayland	148 t.r.
A. v. d. Nieuwenhuizen	149, 188
D. Sander	218
L. Seegers	184
Dr. W. Staeck	120
Tetra-Archiv	10, 15, 19, 24, 27, 33, 39, 42
W. A. Tomey	40/41

Further Reading

Andrews, C.	'A Fishkeepers Guide to Fish Breeding' Salamander/Tetra, 1986
Andrews, C. Exell, A. and Carrington, N.	'Manual of Fish Health' Salamander/Tetra, 1988
James, B.	'A Fishkeepers Guide to Aquarium Plants' Salamander/Tetra, 1986
Loiselle, P.	'The Cichlid Aquarium' Tetra, 1985
Mills, D.	'You and Your Aquarium' Dorling Kindersley, 1986
Mills, D.	'A Popular Guide to Tropical Aquarium Fish' Salamander, 1988
Ramshorst, J. D. van	'The Complete Aquarium Encyclopaedia of Tropical Freshwater Fish' Elsevier-Phaidon, 1978
Sterba, G.	'The Aquarists Encyclopaedia' Blandford, 1983
Whitehead, P.	'How Fishes Live' Elsevier-Phaidon, 1975
Wilkie, D.	'Aquarium Fish' Pelham Books, 1986
Zupanc, G.	'Fish and Their Behaviour' Tetra, 1985